YOU CAN

Pray

IN

TONGUES

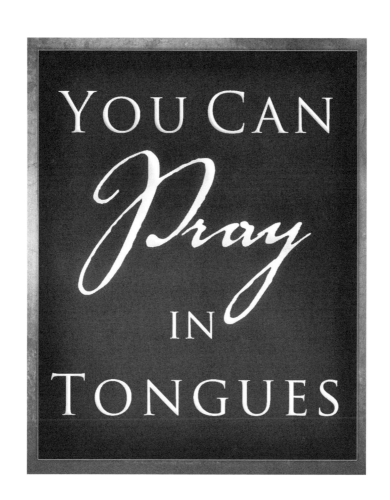

YOU CAN *Pray* IN TONGUES

DON NORI SR.

DESTINY IMAGE® PUBLISHERS, INC.

P.O. Box 310, Shippensburg, PA 17257-0310

"We publish the prophets."

This book and all other Destiny Image, Revival Press, MercyPlace, Fresh Bread, Destiny Image Fiction, and Treasure House books are available at Christian bookstores and distributors worldwide.

For a U.S. bookstore nearest you, call 1-800-722-6774.

For more information on foreign distributors, call 717-532-3040.

Or reach us on the Internet: www.destinyimage.com

ISBN 10: 0-7684-3091-7
ISBN 13: 978-0-7684-3091-2

For Worldwide Distribution, Printed in the U.S.A.
1 2 3 4 5 6 7 8 9 10 11 / 13 12 11 10 09

TABLE OF CONTENTS

INTRODUCTION

A New Day

Today is the beginning of something brand new in your life. You are about to step into a realm of experience and fulfillment that far too few people ever have the opportunity to enjoy. You are about to come face to face with the lover of your soul. The King of kings, the Lord of lords, and your personal friend Jesus Christ, is about to show Himself to you in a way that you have longed for but never really thought was possible.

How can I be so certain of that? I know this for certain because many years ago, I hungered. I hungered for the fullness of the Lord and Him alone. Nothing of this world or religion could satisfy my soul. It was almost out of my control. It was as though He had determined to draw me to Himself and I could do nothing else but yield to Him.

I did not know what it meant, how He was doing it, or what the conclusion of my desire would be. All I knew for certain was that nothing but Jesus Himself would satisfy the longing that burned in my heart.

This ravenous hunger could not be satisfied by the doctrines of mere mortal men or by the works that I was told would most certainly be the answer. I did everything I was taught to try to satisfy my heart. The more people talked, the more I knew the answer was not in humankind. The more I listened to Bible study after Bible study, the more I realized that Jesus alone would be my only answer. He alone could give me what my heart yearned for: fellowship, friendship, union with the living God.

GOD HAD A DREAM FOR ME

Everything earthly, everything correct and acceptable, everything the five senses could be attracted to or titillated by did not hold a candle to what I knew I wanted. I knew I was born for a purpose. I knew there was a dream inside of God's heart for me and, would have no rest until I was sure I was on the path He wanted me to be on. Even after all these years, it is the desire, the continuous hunger for Him that keeps drawing me forward. I go from thirst to fullness, thirst to fullness. I know He walks with me and that Jesus is in me a way that is more real than the body in which I dwell. When I surrendered to Him in the baptism of the Holy Spirit, my heart sang and my spirit soared. I would never, ever be the same again.

Our walk with the Lord, which is the adventure of a lifetime, takes a step forward every time we have a point of surrender to Him. Surrender to the Lord is always the key to progress in our lives. As long as we are surrendered to Him, we experience growth, peace, and a sense of real spiritual adventure. The baptism of the Holy Spirit and praying in tongues is the next step of your personal development and eternal purpose for living.

YOU CAN ONLY IMAGINE

Imagine knowing, beyond a shadow of a doubt, that God hears every prayer. Imagine also that He has determined what you need to pray for and that exact prayer was being prayed as you prayed in tongues. (See Romans 8:26.) Even further, imagine the confidence in that kind of prayer. Imagine the fellowship, the intimacy, the interactive relationship, and the personal reality of knowing you are walking with the living God. No wonder those filled with the Holy Spirit have a great degree of joy, unshakable peace, deep love for the Lord, compassion toward humankind, and desire to serve the Lord in every way. This is the opportunity that praying in tongues presents.

The book you are about to read is not for the intellectual. It is not for the theologian or for the one looking for a passive understanding of the baptism of the Holy Spirit and the deeper Christian life.

THE SEEKER

This book is for the seeker. It is for the one who is hungry of heart and poor of spirit. It is for all those who, in the deepest part of their hearts, know that there is more to the Christian life than any of us were lead to believe. We will spend a lifetime exploring the wonders of the Lord. We will discover His new mercies, new possibilities, and intimate fellowship with Him every day.

The Scripture is clear about praying in tongues:

Anyone who is speaking in an inspired language is not communicating to men, but to God. No one understands him. He is speaking the secrets of God by inspiration (1 Corinthians 14:2).

So lift up the sails of your spirit into the winds of all that is holy and mighty. Lift up your heart and your resolve in faithful anticipation of the next great step in your journey with Jesus through this life. You are about to pray in tongues!

CHAPTER 1

Becoming a Spiritual Person

LEAPING ONTO TROUBLE

I was not looking forward to it. In fact, I did everything I could to get out of it. But it was too late. I had already opened my big mouth about wanting to do more things together. Cathy was quick in her excitement and quick to articulate the first thing she wanted me to do with her. She wanted me to ride a horse. Now you have to understand that, although I love horses, I love them from a distance. Although I had surprised her with two fillies a few years earlier, it had never crossed my mind that I would have to get on these animals someday. I have always been content to keep both feet firmly on the ground. It was way too far from the back of a horse to the ground to suit me.

During the early years, Cathy, being the horse whisperer that she is, trained her two mares with great love, care, and skill, as she had trained so many other horses over the years. But now for the first time in her life, she was training her own horses.

They were awesome animals…from a distance. I was happy to watch her ride. I was even happy to help her in the barn. But then I opened my mouth, and the next minute I was standing beside this huge animal, ready to mount. I needed a stepladder as Black was seventeen hands at the shoulder, which for us non-horse people is about two hundred feet off the ground. I thought I might get a nosebleed from being so high. I even asked Cathy if they made an air bag to wear so a fall would be cushioned. I was not a small man. The thought of sliding off that horse was so frightening. I mean people looked like ants from way up there! I finally was able to convince Cathy to stay on the soft grass instead of the rocky trail, just as a precaution.

Of course Black is a magnificent animal in every way. There was really nothing to be afraid of—at least I tried to tell myself that. I guess I should have been grateful that Cathy was not a skydiver, but at that moment I just wanted out!

Nonetheless, when I saw the excitement on Cathy's face, I knew I wanted to get on that horse and ride with her into the sunset, as long as the sunset was toward the barn. But honestly, my desire to please Cathy was greater than my fear. It is amazing to experience the power of love that causes you to do things that would, under any other circumstances, never be considered.

So, since I am writing this story, it is clear that I did not die and did not fall off (that time!). In fact, I found that riding was as wonderful an experience as Cathy told me it would be. I rode with Cathy in the meadows behind our home. She taught me to ask Black to canter and gallop. It really is like riding the wind, especially on the back of a Tennessee walking horse. We crossed streams and even flushed out pheasant nesting near a bush along a desolate area of railroad tracks.

I don't know what I enjoyed more, the sound of hooves pounding methodically under my feet or Cathy's smile and laughter as we rode. I was glad I took the risk, and I am glad I survived to enjoy it many times over the years. But I had to get over my unfounded fears. When I did, I loved it. I often thought of what I would have missed had I listened to the uncertainty within my own heart. But love broke through all my resistance.

THE HARDEST THINGS MADE EASY

It seems that the hardest things to do can turn out to be the easiest things to do, once we understand them. Being spiritual is one of those things. Since you are reading this, it is safe to say that you want to be spiritual. You want to get close to the Lord. You want to satisfy a hunger that does not seem to go away, no matter what you try. These feelings are evidence of a desire for close, fulfilling fellowship with God. And you are not alone. God made us with a hunger that can only be satisfied with true spirituality. It can only be satisfied with genuine interaction with our Lord Jesus.

The apostle Paul explained this when he said in Romans 8:15-16: *"God did not give you a spirit to make you slaves, to be afraid again. Instead, you received the Spirit who makes you sons. Through the Spirit, we cry out, 'Father, dear Father!' This same Spirit agrees with our spirits, that we are God's children."* I know it is hard to believe, but God wants fellowship with you more than you want it with Him! We have often been taught that God is hard to approach, but He has His arms open to us. He wants us so much that He sent His Son Jesus to become our Savior and King. Since God did not spare His own Son in His rapturous desire for us. He will never withhold anything from us that will bring us closer to Him. If Jesus is alive in your heart, then the next logical step for you to grow in Jesus Christ and into His life is to be filled with the Holy Spirit and begin to pray in tongues.

God's plan for us begins with becoming spiritual people. It is then that we can have true fellowship with Him. That means we begin to hear His Voice more clearly, understand His will for us, change into His likeness and image, become filled with power, and sense His Presence flowing through us in love and all the other fruits of the Spirit.

This is not a difficult way of life; it is path of precious open doors to experience all God has for us and to begin, once and for all, to find fulfillment in our lives.

WHERE DO WE FIND HIM?

The apostle John once quoted Jesus as saying, *"You are always searching the Scriptures, because you think you will find eternal life in them. But the Scriptures are giving proof about Me!"* (John 5:39).

Humans look for the Lord in many places, but fulfillment is found only in Him, and He is found in the Spirit where He lives. We can learn all about Him, but that does not mean we know Him. We can memorize all the Scriptures and follow all the rules we are told to follow. But we will always end up being hungry and, I may add, frustrated.

Why is it that we can do everything we are told to do and still not be fulfilled? There is a simple answer for most people. It is because we are spiritual people. Our fulfillment is meant to come from the realm of the Spirit. It is the Spirit that truly feeds the soul. It is the soul that truly rules the heart. It is the heart that emboldens us to do the impossible and experience life on the highest plane of existence.

We are spiritual people. We were always meant to communicate fellowship, discern, and live in the spiritual realm. Fellowship with a system of rules is not fellowship in the Holy Spirit. It is in the Spirit that the life of God pours into every fiber of our being. It is the Spirit that softens our hearts, strengthens our souls, and gives us the courage to not just survive, but to triumph. When we fellowship with the real living Person of Jesus Christ, our hearts begin to be fulfilled.

I can remember the early days of my search. I did not care about anything but satisfying my deep spiritual hunger. I was almost too afraid to think about it, though, for I feared that there was no way to ever actually find resolution. I thought I was doomed to a life of silent misery and unfulfillment. Even though my religious upbringing required so much, it delivered so little.

To me, it was not enough to be at church twice a week and follow the myriad of rules and laws. None of these brought any satisfaction. I thought I was really offtrack because these activities never brought true fulfillment. I was haunted by the thought that I would never measure up to the standards that were presented to me by religion. I just could not do it.

Although I wanted more than anything else to belong to Him and know that I was pleasing Him, it just did not seem possible. Even worse, I thought that maybe Jesus just didn't like me or that He was too busy for me. Of all the things He had to keep track of, I was certain that *my* needs and heart-felt desires were far down on His priority list.

But now I understand. Nothing could be further from the truth. Think of this for a moment. God is so big that He can give all of Himself to each one of us. That won't seem so strange when you realize that parents give all of themselves to every child. It is the capacity of the heart that counts. God's love is profoundly eternal, far more capable of love than our human minds can comprehend. He gathers and gathers and gathers some more. We are not time wasters to Him. We are not His second choice. He is so big that He focuses all love and attention on each one of us without slighting anyone.

Understanding and truly experiencing this with the Lord is one function of the Spirit realm. When we see Him for who

He is, everything changes. Our picture is enlarged and our faith grows, never again to return to the way things were.

LOVE FROM ANOTHER DIMENSION

Something eternal, something *otherworldly, other-dimensional* is planted deep within our hearts when we see Him in the Spirit. Nothing is the same again.

Once you have seen Him, once you have touched the invisible, it is impossible to go back to the way things were. The religious systems of today cannot begin to compare to the wonders of what is available in the realm of the Spirit, where the possibilities are endless of fulfilling the dream God has for you.

Blaise Pascal, the French philosopher made this statement:

There is a God shaped vacuum in the heart of every man which cannot be filled by any created thing, but only by God, the Creator, made known through Jesus.

The natural man can *never* satisfy the spirit man. God intended it that way so we would search for Him where He is, in the Spirit—not in Heaven, but in the Spirit.

There is a great Oliver Wendell Holmes quote that I can never forget and it relates here:

One's mind, once stretched by a new idea, never regains its original dimensions.

We can never force out of our mind what has been placed there by the Spirit of God. We then become responsible for that truth, and we can never live our lives without that thought encroaching upon our consciousness.

The solution is not hard, nor is it far from your grasp. God is looking for spiritual people. He is looking for people just like you. For true spirituality brings union with Him, union with His purposes, union with His desires.

Some people who do not believe in the Spirit still crave inner fulfillment, but many of these people think they can force fulfillment by going to the extreme limits with the body. So they experiment with drugs, alcohol, sex, bizarre risk-taking, body building, etc. Humanity, left to its own devices, will always look for anything that might touch the emptiness and hunger that is inherent deep in our hearts.

You will never nurture your spiritual needs with things from the natural dimension. You can do great service for your fellow man or woman. You can give away riches or dedicate your life to the poor, but it will not satisfy the soul. Spiritual things are nurtured by spiritual things. That is why praying in tongues is so important. It is spiritual water for the soul.

KING DAVID PEERED INTO ETERNITY

King David was a man with many questions. He did not understand why so many injustices were left unpunished and even prospered. He did not like the oppression of the poor and the orphan. He hated deception and treachery of all kinds. He complained to the Lord about these things. He did not understand until he entered the sanctuary of the Lord, which is a type of His Presence, the spirit realm. *"I tried to understand all of this, but it was too much for me to stand, **until** I went to the sanctuary of God! **Then** I understood what will happen to them"* (Ps. 73:16-17). When David peered into eternity, his world changed, his attitudes changed, his understanding of people changed. For the first time, he saw the spirit realm. He saw that it controls, enslaves, teaches, or heals, depending upon whom you are seeking and whom you find in the spirit dimension. Martin Luther once said, "Faith takes you where reason alone cannot take you."

When we see into other dimensions, we understand so much more; for we are multidimensional people, designed to live and function inter-dimensionally. In fact, our five natural senses are intended to connect us with this physical dimension only. Anything from another dimension is naturally rejected. The human mind will never comprehend the things that cannot be explored, explained, or proven by the five senses.

The five senses simply are not designed to discern the things of the spirit and report those things to the mind. The five senses report taste, color, sound, touch, and smell. The spirit of a person reports the things of the spirit realm. Those spiritual senses are delivered to the mind for analysis, just as our senses deliver their information to our minds. But since we are trained to reject anything that cannot be touched by at least one of our natural senses, these spiritual senses are either ignored or outright rejected.

This is where science makes its fatal error. Science demands that everything must be verifiable by at least one of the five senses. Therefore, all dimensions of existence must submit to the dimension in which we live in order to be accepted.

Of course, it is this typical human arrogance that demands all life submit to humanity's rules of engagement, no matter how archaic and closed-minded those rules may be. Religion, in general, has done the same thing over the years. Even as the human spirit has craved fulfillment, the self-appointed powers of religion and science determine what is real and what is not real. Every dimension has its reality. The adventurer within will explore and discover the wonders of these realities.

The more honest we are with ourselves, the more likely we are to eventually accept the things that go on around us that cannot be touched by our natural senses. For the unseen world is filled with activity! Our willingness to live one-dimensionally will inhibit, if not completely prevent a dynamic, interactive relationship with God. Our faith is really the knowledge that more exists than what we have been taught to accept. What is invisible to the natural eye is visible to the spirit of a person. Faith allows you to see what cannot otherwise be seen. (See Second Corinthians 4:18.)

PEOPLE OF SPIRIT

Like King David, we must enter the sanctuary of God, the realm of spirit, to perceive their end (see Ps. 73:16-17). When we see in the spirit realm, we can see and experience worlds that most only dream about.

But there is a great cautionary note necessary here. There is a vast difference between being in the spirit realm and being in the Spirit. *In the Spirit,* describes what I like to call the realm of *all-God*. This is a place in the Spirit of God where He dwells in all His fullness. To simply conduct a séance or play with anything that conjures spirits will open you to some very nasty, very evil stuff. That is why our prayers always need to be in the Name of Jesus. When we meditate on the Scriptures or the Lord, we do it with an open heart to the Holy Spirit alone. When the Scriptures talk about being *in the Spirit,* they refer to the Spirit of God. Here are some examples:

*However, **you** are not being controlled by human nature; you are being controlled by the Spirit—if God's Spirit lives in you…* (Romans 8:9).

…But you were washed of sin and made holy. You have been made right with God by the authority of the Lord Jesus Christ and with the Spirit of our God (1 Corinthians 6:11).

Pray with the Spirit at all times. Use all kinds of prayers and requests. Be on guard! Always pray for all the holy people (Ephesians 6:18).

During the Lord's day, I was in the Spirit. I heard a loud voice speaking behind me. It was like the sound from a trumpet (Revelation 1:10).

YOUR OPEN INVITATION

*"I am the way and the truth and the life! The only way anyone can come to the Father is through **Me!*** (John 14:6). These words of Jesus offer the most exciting invitation we could receive. He has opened the doors of eternity, of the spirit realm, for us to enter and enjoy. The apostle tells us that we are raised up with Him, and Jesus seated us *"in the heavenly world with Christ Jesus"* (Eph. 2:6)—those heavenly places resting with Him in the Spirit, from which flow all life and completeness.

One of the most important passages concerning spirituality can be found in John 4:23-24: *"But the time is coming and has now come when the true worshipers will worship the Father in the true, spiritual way. The Father is searching for this kind of people to worship Him. God is spirit. The people who worship God must worship Him in the true way and with the right spirit."* His arms are open and He is awaiting our willingness to step into our destiny as spiritual people.

In this instance, your heart gives you away. You are reading what you hope will be the answer to what you are searching for. I want to assure you that this is what God has for you and for all those who call on Him.

It is an amazing miracle. God has prepared a place in the spirit realm where you can be spiritual while you are still natural. Your five senses put you in touch with the natural things of life, but your spirit puts you in touch with the spiritual things of life. When you are not spiritual, you miss most of God's wonderful creation since He has created both the natural as well as the spiritual realm.

Let us no longer be satisfied with being only half a person. Let us give ourselves to Him that He may bring us into the realm of the Spirit, the realm of *all-God*, where real communion begins and real fulfillment is the conclusion.

Is Anyone Thirsty?

Because the Holy Spirit is a real Person with thoughts, love, and power, our interactive relationship with Him is as real as our relationship with anyone else. Living *in Him* is literally living with the realm, the borders, the castle of *all-God*. Here His Presence is like a continuous flow of cool water on a hot day, refreshing our souls and bringing new hopes and dreams within our hearts to life.

"Any person who drinks this water will become thirsty again, but if anyone drinks the water which I will give him, he will never be thirsty again. The water which I give him will become a spring inside him, welling up to eternal life." (John 4:13-14). Here Jesus is talking to a young woman who went to the well to draw water. Jesus is showing her the difference between natural water and spiritual water (Holy Spirit). When we begin to draw from the Spirit, we will never thirst again. Natural water from the well is a type of sweaty, human effort to find thirst-quenching reality. But Jesus offered another kind of water, His Spirit, of which this woman could drink and never thirst for fulfillment again.

Once the Holy Spirit begins to move within your heart and you move in the heart of God, fulfillment will be a daily, powerful, loving experience.

CHAPTER
2

It Never Ended

Jesus Christ is the same yesterday, today, and forever (Hebrews 13:8).

GOD DOESN'T CHANGE

The Gospel is full of good news. But the best news of all the good news is that God never changes. In a world where everything seems to change, we can be certain that God never changes. His heart's desire toward us is as strong and committed as it can be. No mathematical equation can calculate His love; for

He loves to the infinite power of eternity. Nothing can change it, nothing can slow it down, and nothing can break it. Of this we can be certain.

He is, and always will be, the active participant for good in our lives. But contemporary believers are not the first people to wonder if God ever changes. The writer of Hebrews talked about this very thing nearly 2,000 years ago:

> *God wanted to show very clearly that His plan would not change. So, He made a vow to confirm it to the people who received the promise made to Abraham. It is impossible for God to lie about these two actions. God wanted to use these two things (which cannot change) to give us much comfort. We have run for safety to take hold of the hope that is in front of us. This hope that we have is like an anchor for the soul. It is safe and sure. It goes behind the curtain inside the heavenly temple sanctuary* (Hebrews 6:17-19).

The same promises He gave to the fathers thousands of years ago are our promises today. They are just as true and just as powerful today. Nothing has changed. We do not serve a god of the past or a god of the dead, but we serve a living God who always delivers on His promises.

When He makes a promise, He keeps it.

When Peter preached immediately after he was filled with the Holy Spirit on that first Pentecost after Jesus rose from the dead, he made it clear that God's plan was for men and women of all time. Peter, under divine inspiration, saw that everyone could and should be filled with the Holy Spirit. Check out a portion of his first Pentecostal sermon here:

> *Then Peter answered, "Change your hearts and each one of you must be immersed by the authority of Jesus the Messiah, so that your sins may be forgiven. Then you will receive the gift of the Holy Spirit"* (Acts 2:38).

Now, here is the awesome verse we need to see: *"This promise is for you and for your children. It is also for people who are far away, for everyone whom the Lord our God may call"* (Acts 2:39). Peter could see far into the future. But as far as he could look, he could not see an end to this wonderful promise. As God opened his eyes to see the ages to come, all he could see were people of every tribe, tongue, and continent being filled with the Holy Spirit. No wonder everyone around Peter thought he was drunk. He was drunk in the Holy Spirit. He was filled to overflowing. His physical body could barely stand the power and could not contain the Presence. Outsiders looked at him with natural eyes and thought he was drunk. But Peter was quick to tell the onlookers that although they were outsiders, with repentance they could quickly become insiders and enjoy the experience of a lifetime.

WHO RECEIVED THE HOLY SPIRIT?

The Bible tells us that all kinds of people have received the Holy Spirit and prayed in tongues. In fact, we find that when the Holy Spirit was first poured out, people of all races and nationalities received the Holy Spirit and prayed in tongues. God does not like one person better than another. If your heart is open, He will fill you with His Spirit, as He did on that first Pentecostal outpouring that is explained in the Book of Acts. All the apostles and 120 others were gathered together to pray and wait for the promise that Jesus said He would bring. In Acts 1 verse 8, after He was raised from the dead and just before He ascended into Heaven, Jesus promised this to His disciples: *"When the Holy Spirit comes upon you, you will receive power. You will be my witnesses in Jerusalem, in all of Judea, in Samaria, and to the farthest parts of the world"* (Acts 1:8).

This is very important because the Lord Jesus knew that the disciples would not be able to be witnesses and do the work of the ministry in their own strength, so He promised them power to preach the Gospel to *remotest parts of the earth.*

The ages since that first Pentecost have been filled with the records of literally millions who have received this same experience. Believers have relied on this power as they courageously brought the Gospel to the four corners of the earth. The power of the Holy Spirit was with them as they preached, healed the sick, restored the brokenhearted, cured the lame, and raised the dead. Demons are cast out and the poor have the Gospel preached to them by this magnificent power.

The truth is that outside the USA, speaking and praying in tongues goes across denominational lines and is a common experience in the lives of most Christians. In fact, speaking and praying in tongues is considered a necessity in nearly every country of the world.

Mennonites, Lutherans, Methodists, Amish, Nazarenes, Episcopalians, Presbyterians, Orthodox, Baptists, Roman Catholics, and many, many others speak and pray in tongues every day. In fact, among most groups where Jesus Christ is confessed as Savior and Lord, you will find those who speak and pray in tongues.

This incredible miracle that is awaiting you has never changed. It has never been altered and the evidence of it is monumental. It is this same power, this same Spirit, this same promise that awaits you as you prepare your heart and your understanding to receive the Holy Spirit and begin to pray in tongues.

The promise is for all those who are open to receive. It is not for an elite group or special people; for we are all special in His eyes. It is not just for leaders or evangelists. It is not only for those who are missionaries into Africa. It is for the priesthood of the Lord, which includes all who are believers. Peter understood who we are when he wrote,

> But **you** are a chosen race, a royal group of priests, a holy nation, and a special people. You must tell about the wonderful things that God has done. He called you from darkness into His amazing light. The Scripture says: "Those who were once not a people are now God's people. Those who had not received mercy now have received mercy." (1 Peter 2:9-10).

WHO GOD CALLS

God does not segregate based on position, income, popularity, ministry, or name. He does withhold His power due to our weakness and insecurity. In fact, He loves to confuse and baffle the wise among us by giving Himself to those who don't think much of themselves. He knows these people will be perfect candidates to carry His Presence to a dying world. He understands that those who know they are needy will be soft and quiet before the Lord and listen most intently to His voice. God knows that the meek will certainly inherit the earth (see Matt. 5:5) and He will be sure to give them the power to do so. His heart is toward you and He will fill you with His Spirit. John the Baptist explained it this way:

> *Whenever you change your hearts, I immerse you in water. But there is one coming later who is more important than I am. I am not worthy to carry His shoes. **He will immerse you in the Holy Spirit and in fire!*** (Matthew 3:11).

This is how it happened the first time. But remember, your experience will be different. God does not always repeat Himself when He fills someone with the Holy Spirit. Here are the specifics of Peter's account of what happened that day:

> *When the day of Pentecost came, they were all together in one place. Suddenly, a noise came from the sky. It sounded like a strong wind blowing. This noise filled the whole house where they were sitting. They saw something which looked like flames of fire separating and staying over each one of them. They were all filled with the Holy Spirit and they began to speak different inspired languages; the Spirit was giving them the power to do this. There were some devout Jewish men staying in Jerusalem at this time. These men were from every country in the world. A large group of them came together because they heard the noise. They were confused. The apostles were speaking, and every man heard in his own language. The Jewish people were all*

amazed at this. They didn't understand how the apostles could do this. They said, "Look! These men whom we hear speaking are all from Galilee! But each of us is hearing them in our own native language. We are: Parthians, Medes, Elamites, those living in Mesopotamia, from Judea, from Cappodocia, from Pontus, from Asia, from Phrygia, from Pamphylia, from Egypt, from parts of Libya around Cyrene, visitors from Rome, Cretans, Arabians. Some of us were born Jews. Others are converts to Judaism. We can hear these men in our own languages! We can all understand the wonderful things they are saying about God" (Acts 2:1-11).

Just imagine having an experience like that! Imagine the power of the Holy Spirit so strong and powerful that you appeared to be drunk! The world changed for these 120 people, and it will change for you too. These people were filled with the Spirit of God Himself and with all the love and peace they could contain. From that one event, the Gospel rocketed throughout the known world. There was no television, no satellite, no email, no iPod, no mobile phone, and no books! Yet the power of the Holy Spirit was all that was needed to proclaim the limitless love of God to the nations.

God loves to give Himself to hungry believers just like you. He knows that this is exactly what you need at this point in your Christian life. That is why you are reading this.

There is something inside of you (the Holy Spirit) urging you on, stirring your heart, and convincing you that He is calling you closer to Him.

WHO IS WORTHY?

There are many people who feel that they are not worthy. They think that they have to attain to a high degree of holiness before they can receive the Holy Spirit. Others believe that the Holy Spirit is a reward for serving the Lord. Still others will say that the baptism of the Holy Spirit is reserved for those who are especially spiritual and gifted. I know many who think that it is too hard to receive or that they are living in too much sin to receive.

But here is more good news: The baptism of the Holy Spirit is not a reward for being good, holy, or spiritual. The truth is that the baptism of the Holy Spirit is a tool, not a reward. Its purpose is to change you, empower you, and strengthen you to become all that your heavenly Father has dreamed for you to become.

We traveled once to a small church to minister. We were a bit shocked at how well we were treated. But soon we became very uncomfortable with our treatment. We felt almost like we were being worshiped. It soon became evident why we were being treated as we were. Somewhere in their history, the people had been taught that only an elect few would ever have the honor of being baptized with the Holy Spirit. Most never thought they would ever actually meet someone who had received the Holy Spirit, let alone experience it for themselves. Well, it turned out to be an awesome visit as we gave them the good news of the free gift of God. They joyfully, and may I say ecstatically, received! These are people who will absolutely never be the same again.

But thinking that the baptism of the Holy Spirit is a reward is not new. There was a time in the Book of Acts, when the believers, who were all Jewish, did not believe that non-Jews were able to be Christians. It actually never crossed their minds to evangelize anyone but Jews. Then, Peter was invited to a Gentile (non-Jewish) home to preach. As Peter spoke to them about God's love and the resurrection of Jesus Christ from the dead, he was amazed that the Holy Spirit fell on everyone in the room. None of them were Jews; yet, they began to speak in tongues under the power of the Holy Spirit just as the Jewish believers had experienced.

That event changed Peter's thinking as well as the faith as they had defined it. For now, the salvation of the Lord Jesus and the baptism of the Holy Spirit were not just for Jews, but all men as well. Peter rightly concluded that since the Holy Spirit had been given to Gentiles by the Lord Jesus, they could not possibly be refused fellowship. Peter's heart expanded that day to include all people.

There is something in humanity that wants to separate rather than gather. We seem to always build walls between instead of walls around us as a whole. God will always break down the things that divide us so we can be of one mind in Christ.

I was once an assistant pastor of a vibrant and growing Charismatic church not far from our home. Our doors and our hearts were always open to the downtrodden and weary. Cathy and I had, and still have, particularly open hearts when it comes to this kind of person since we have also experienced very difficult times over the years. So when a small family came into the church one Sunday morning, we knew God was giving us an opportunity to show His love to them.

There were many things about this small family that are not pertinent to the story. But they were in need and we were there for them. As was my custom, I went to the altar after the service to pray for those who wanted it. On this particular Sunday, this young family came forward for prayer.

In just a short time, I discovered that they were already believers but knew nothing about the Holy Spirit. I took some time to explain the power of the Holy Spirit and how He would help them to overcome seemingly insurmountable obstacles in their lives. There were only a few people left in the church when Cathy and I began to pray for them. They were instantly filled with the Holy Spirit and began to pray in tongues. It is difficult to describe the relief in their eyes as they prayed and prayed, alternately laughing and crying as the Lord began the inner healing process in their lives.

It was an amazing and wonderful day for them. They continued to attend the meetings, and the growth in their lives was quite obvious. Even the children were happier. We watched with excited thankfulness as this small family was changed right before our eyes.

A few weeks later I received a call from the senior pastor who had some disturbing news. It seems that the local authorities were looking for the couple for having fraudulently received an energy assistance check for their home. In the course of the conversation it was learned that the couple we had prayed for were not married. The two children were theirs. They had been together nearly five years.

The senior pastor scolded me, saying that I had acted in haste when I offered to pray for them. "You laid hands on them and prayed for them to receive the baptism of the Holy Spirit without doing any research. Now we have a problem."

I asked him, "What is the problem? The Holy Spirit will..." but before I could finish my statement, he interrupted by saying,

"The problem is that you baptized these people in the Holy Spirit while they are still in sin. They are speaking in tongues while they are living together outside of marriage."

Since I was not in a position of authority, I had to stand by and watch as this couple was shamed out of the church.

GOD SEES OUR HEARTS

I wonder how many people are denied the opportunity of being filled with the Spirit because of sin that is in their lives. I don't know anyone who is free of sin. But most importantly, the Holy Spirit gives power to help overcome sin in our lives. We will never, ever be pure enough in ourselves to be worthy of His Spirit within us.

That is the power of forgiveness. He forgives us. He washes us clean of the effects of sin on our lives and He is the One who gives Himself to anyone who is a Christian, regardless of their current condition. To be sure, the Lord will not allow someone to continue in sin, but it is the Holy Spirit who will tell us and help us through every situation to become free. Our Lord looks at the heart and deals with us according to the condition of the heart. My role is not to judge, but to open the heavenly doorway of opportunity to all who ask. He knows the sound and condition of His sheep, and He will bring everyone who is soft of heart and broken in spirit to Himself.

JESUS IS THE BAPTIZER

But here is something even more important. I cannot baptize anyone in the Holy Spirit. That is the ministry of Jesus and Jesus alone. Remember what John the Baptist said about Jesus?

> *Whenever you change your hearts, I* [John] *immerse you in water. But there is one* [Jesus] *coming later who is more important than I am. I am not worthy to carry His shoes. He will immerse you in the Holy Spirit and in fire!* (Matthew 3:11)

I can pray for someone all day long, but if the Lord does not want to fill that person, he or she won't be filled. But that is the point; the Holy Spirit cleanses, delivers, frees, heals, restores, and leads. The baptism of the Holy Spirit is a tool to bring each believer into his or her destiny. He does not withhold Himself because He knows how we are made; and He knows that we need His Spirit to not only live in Christ, but to be victorious in Him in a supernatural way.

No, the baptism of the Holy Spirit is not a reward but a vital tool in our walk with Jesus. It is a tool that will forever change your life and give you real hope for your future and the future of all those you love so dearly.

Jesus never instituted lifeless rituals into His Church. Everything He commands, He commands because we need it. The door is open and He is waiting to equip you with the most awesome tool of growth, power, and change the universe has to offer. He is offering it to you!

CHAPTER
3

This Is What Happened to Me

I had discovered the incredible love of God toward me personally just three weeks earlier. Before that time, I had resigned myself to what I believed would always be a one-way love and one-way desire. I figured that I would love and serve the Lord as best as I could but He would never love me enough for me to be able to make Him happy in return. Life became one failure after another as I tried to face the future with the love of my life, Jesus. But when I found God loved me even more than I loved Him, absolutely everything changed.

Discovering His indescribable and eternal love for me was almost too much to expect. Nonetheless, I knew my experience was real. In fact, I never thought to question it. That was the extent of the change in my heart, my attitude, and my outlook for the future. I knew in my heart of hearts that no matter what anyone would ever say to me, Jesus' promise to me was this, *"My sheep listen to My voice. I know them. They follow Me. I give them eternal life. They will **never** be lost. No one will snatch them out of My hand"* (John 10:27-28).

Jesus' words gave me the strength and confidence to believe Him before I would believe anyone else. I had spent years doing precisely what I was told to do with the assurance that everything would turn out the way I wanted it to. But I discovered that things only turned out the way everyone else wanted things to turn out. I knew it was time I did what my heart was pressing me to do. I had to press through my fears and doubt; and He was with me at every point of decision.

This particular evening I was walking across the campus of Shippensburg University, where I earned my degrees. I was returning from a wonderful evening with other believers, talking and praying together. It was just after midnight. I was thinking about my new life and how everything was changing. I had heard about praying in tongues and I had asked the Lord if that was something He wanted me to do. But thus far I was too timid to ask anyone for help.

As I walked in front of the campus library on that foggy, fateful evening, a song began to well up in my spirit. This was strange, as I did not seem to know what I was singing. It was as though I had never heard the song. Suddenly I realized that I was singing in an unknown tongue! My spirit leaped in worship, and my hands flew into the air. I was so glad there was no one around as I am sure I looked quite crazy. But I could not help it! The union with the Lord that I felt...no...that I knew I had...was just overwhelming. I sang, I cried, I laughed. I walked, I ran, and I jumped. I simply could not contain what was happening to me. God was flooding me, immersing me, cleansing me, healing me with His Spirit. The weeks, months, and years to follow would be a process of growth and restoration that began in earnest that incredible autumn night in 1972.

I HAD HOPE

For the first time in a very, very long time, I felt cared for, safe, and hopeful. Things were going to be different— not because I alone was determined to change, but because there was Someone inside of me who was determined to change me and fulfill all that I was born to do. For the first time in my life, I had hope that I was born for a purpose. I began to realize that God dreamed a dream for me before I was ever born. He held that dream in His heart until the time when I would open myself to Him and really let Him have His will done in my life. I was finally in safe hands and I knew it by experience, not just because someone told me.

I went back to my room and lay on my bed, praying and singing in tongues. The strength of His Presence was something I had not experienced before that night. The more I prayed in tongues, the more comfortable I was with it. I discovered I could pray in tongues in my mind without uttering a word with my mouth. I discovered that the more I prayed, the more I wanted to pray. My prayer language grew stronger and stronger. It wasn't long before I felt completely comfortable with this experience and I loved praying in tongues.

I opened my Bible and found that even the Word came alive in a way that I never thought possible. Jesus was…no…*is* so real! That reality was something I could not, and still cannot, intellectually understand. I just *knew* He was all the Bible said He was. For the first time I understood what the apostle meant when he said, *"Since we are children, we are also heirs—heirs of God and co-heirs with Christ…"* (Rom. 8:17).

The Holy Spirit was showing me the things that Jesus taught in the Bible. To this day, I am awestruck at the revelation of Jesus through the Holy Scriptures. The apostle John prepared us for this when he relayed Jesus' message: "I will send you the Comforter from the Father. He is the Spirit of truth who is coming out from the Father. When He comes, He will tell the truth about Me" (John 15:26).

Jesus also said, *"I will ask My Father and He will give you another Comforter—the Spirit of truth. He will be with you forever. The people of the world cannot accept Him, because they don't see Him or know Him, but you know Him because He stays with you—He is in you. I will not abandon you, as though you were orphans. I am coming to you"* (John 14:16-18).

HE BECAME MY STRENGTH

To be sure, the future was wrought with difficulty, trouble, and mistakes, but I knew that He was the God of great patience, mercy, and forgiveness. As often as I messed up, He would forgive me and urge me forward. I knew it. I experienced it. He gave me strength and I was beginning to hear Him speak to me and restore my soul. I began to discover how much there was to see in the realm of *all-God*. The Holy Spirit was teaching me, showing me, leading me. I began the lifelong adventure of eternal discovery. I am still learning and exploring this great God we serve, and He is as exciting now—37 years later—as He has ever been.

> *I still have many things to tell you, but you cannot take it right now. When the Spirit of truth comes, He will guide you*

into all truth. He will not speak on His own authority. He will say whatever He hears. He will tell you about things to come. He will give Me glory. He will take what I am saying and will tell it to you. Everything that belongs to my Father belongs to Me, too. This is why I said, "He will take what I am saying and tell it to you."...Jesus said, "In a little while, you will not see Me anymore, but then, after a little while, you will see Me!" (John 16:12-14,16).

YOU NEED TO KNOW

I share my story here for a few reasons. It is important that you realize how committed God is and how multifaceted He is. You need to know that He is determined to give you joy, deep inner satisfaction, and destiny.

EVERYONE IS GOD'S FAVORITE

First, I want you to understand that everyone is truly God's favorite. He loves us all the same. I was a loser of the highest measure, but God never saw me that way. He saw me and sees me now according to His love and His plan for me. Even after all these years, God is dreaming dreams for me and laying out paths of purpose and fulfillment.

He is waiting to open the blessings of Heaven for you and in you. He wants to talk to you and show you His love by experience, not just in words. He wants you to have a daily experience of His Presence that is both tangible as well as fulfilling. Life is never boring, nor is it aimless. For He sets you on a direction of effectiveness in all you do and say. As He shows the things of the Spirit, your words are full of wisdom and hope; for you begin to see things from His perspective, as they really are.

THERE IS NO COMPARISON

Second, everyone's experience will be different. The stories of how and when someone first spoke and prayed in tongues are as varied as the people who experience them. Some are filled with the Spirit in the quiet of their own homes. Some will receive as they are being prayed for by others. Some sing in tongues before they speak in tongues. Some hear the tongue in their minds before they speak it out with their voices. Still others speak in tongues in their dreams. Some are emotional while others have no emotion at all. Some whisper at first, while others cry when they first begin to speak. I have heard hundreds of stories over my 37 years of walking with the Lord.

YOUR FAITH GROWS

Third—and this is awesome, indeed. It is the next step in experiencing a close relationship with the Lord that is interactive and rewarding on an emotional, spiritual, and natural level. This step is where our faith goes to a higher level of communion and involvement with the activity of the Holy Spirit. Our relationship is now a two-way relationship. He hears us and we hear Him. He leads us and we follow. He teaches us how to pray and we pray that way. God is *with* us. He is not one who receives our prayers as one receives an e-mail. He is not *up there* somewhere. As the Scripture says so beautifully, *"The Always-Present One is near everyone who calls out to Him,"* (Ps. 145:18).

NOW YOU KNOW

Now you know that you know that you know: He is near you. He is in you. He knows. He understands and His Spirit is at work on your behalf and on behalf of the ones for whom you pray. There is no begging, no claiming, no reminding, no worrying. He is as good as His Word.

> *...I will make what I have said come true. I will do what I have planned* (Isaiah 46:11).

*The God of peace Himself will make you completely holy. May He keep your spirit, soul, and body whole without guilt until our Lord Jesus Christ comes. And, He **will** come. God is the One who calls you. He is faithful* (1 Thessalonians 5:23-24).

*"I say this because I know what I have planned for you," says the Always-Present One. "I have good plans for you. I do **not** plan to hurt you. I plan to give you hope and a good future. Then you will call on My Name. You will come to Me and pray to Me. And, I will listen to you. You will search for Me. And, when you search for Me with all your heart, you will find Me! I will let you find Me," says the Always-Present One. "And I will bring you back from your captivity. I forced you to leave this place. But I will gather you from all the nations. I will gather you from the places where I have sent you as captives," says the Always-Present One, "And, I will bring you back to this place"* (Jeremiah 29:11-14).

CHAPTER
4

Who Can Do It?

A GOD OF RELATIONSHIP

Who does God want to bless? Who is worthy? Who is righteous? Who is good enough to receive all the things God has for us? We all know that the heavens are overflowing with blessing and purpose. The Spirit oozes with destiny. But how to access all this seems to be elusive to many people. There are books by the thousands filled with formulas and procedures intended to open the floodgates of Heaven upon us. But the heart and soul of God's participation in the affairs of humankind have nothing to do with methods of spiritual success. It has everything to do with relationship. We serve a God of relationship. This fellowship with God, in itself, opens the heavens just as your marriage relationship opens the floodgates of fulfillment for both husband and wife.

Nonetheless, it is difficult for the believer to accept this. It seems too easy, too elementary to be for real. Deep inside we reason—we know who we are and we know these blessings will not come. But there are reasons we feel this way, and it is the problem we face.

I NEVER LIKED WHAT I SAW

If you are like most people, you are preoccupied with your failures. They always seem to be right in front of us. We want to serve God and be pleasing to Him, but it just does not seem possible. So the conclusion is obvious: Why would God give me anything when I am so weak and unable to be what I should be?

I used to get up every morning and face the most depressing sight I could imagine—myself in the mirror! It was not so much because of how I looked that early in the morning; we all secretly know it takes some preparation before we want to be seen by anyone!

Instead, for me, looking at myself in the mirror caused me to remember all the ways I fell short of His glory and, hence, His favor. It was a truly a pathetic site. I would remember all the things that I was not, as well as all the things I wanted to be. I would always conclude that I would have to be satisfied with the truth. That truth was that I would always be a failure and that there was nothing I could do about it. It was easy to look around at my friends and fellow believers and envy them for their apparent success next to my failure. "I will never be like them," I would lament to myself. "I will never measure up to the standard of life I see in them."

That thought would be followed by a big sigh of resignation. My day would begin on that awful note. I am sure you can imagine what it is like trying to do your best as a husband, father, mother, wife, son, or daughter and still feeling as though you have not been all you could be. It was nearly impossible to pull myself out of that feeling long enough to accomplish anything I wanted to do that day. All my strength, all my thoughts, and all my time was spent trying to battle through such feelings of depression, failure, and hopelessness. It seemed as though all the wonderful promises in the Scriptures concerning the triumphant life of the believer would never include me.

It was not that I did not try, but I always seemed to end up pretending I was someone else. The real me hid inside, struggling for any kind of hope and peace, while on the outside, I put on the front of being happy and fulfilled. I knew better than to tell someone of my struggle. After all, we are supposed to be fulfilled, but I was not. We are supposed to be able to hear the voice of the Lord, but I did not. I was supposed to be able to have the strength to move mountains and change the world. But I could not muster the strength to make it through the day! How would I ever change the world? By the end of the day I was normally exhausted and more frustrated than ever. I couldn't wait to just fall asleep and forget the struggle for a few hours.

It was not that I did not live in repentance. I repented several times a day, even when I did not do anything wrong. I was continually haunted by the thought that God did not like me. I asked His forgiveness 100 times each week, just trying to get rid of the guilt that echoed in my heart and mind from morning to night.

There was a wall between myself and my Lord. I loved Him so much yet it seemed as though He did not return that love. I loved Him because, well, I don't know why. I just loved Him and wanted Him to love and accept me as I did Him. It seemed that He would never really love me. He would only accept me. Furthermore, He would only accept me if I acted exactly the way I was expected to act and if I did all the things I was told to do. So it wasn't really love at all. In fact I didn't even think it was acceptance, but rather *toleration.* That's it. He tolerated me if I did all the right things and I was a good person. What kind of love relationship can you have with someone like that? None. I guarantee it!

I think the worst part was the guilt I always carried. I felt guilty because I never felt satisfied with my life as a believer in Jesus. I knew I was supposed to be satisfied but I wasn't. I felt like such a heretic! How could I have the Lord in the fullness of His Presence and still feel like I lacked joy and fulfillment? Isn't that the worst insult to the Lord that anyone could offer? I knew I could not just go tell someone that God was not fulfilling, so I suffered in the silence of my own heart. There was no help. I just fell short of what I expected of myself and I fell short, or so I thought, of what God expected from me.

WHO IS OUR TEACHER?

But then something remarkable began to happen. I began to see verses in the Bible that contradicted what I had been taught for so many years. I began to get a picture of the Lord that was not reflected in anything I had read or in anything I had heard preached. I began to discover a God I always hoped existed but never found. I found the God of forgiveness and the God of mercy.

When I began to find Scriptures that contradicted what I thought and what I had been taught, I had a dilemma. Who was I going to believe? Who would I give control of my heart? Who would always have my best interest when teaching me? Who could I even trust to teach me? These were very hard questions, but they demanded an answer as I searched my heart and prayed for guidance.

Finally the answer began to emerge when I read the apostle John's first letter:

> *God gave you a gift. You still have this gift inside you. You don't need anyone to teach you. The gift that He gave you teaches you about everything. This gift is true; it is not false. Because of this, continue to live in God, just as His gift taught you* (1 John 2:27).

Then I found what Jesus said about being taught:

> *The Comforter will teach you everything. He will cause you to remember everything I have told you. He is the Holy Spirit. The Father will send Him with My authority* (John 14:26).

> *You should not be called 'Rabbi,' because there is only one teacher for you. You are all brothers* (Matthew 23:8).

> *Since I, the Lord and Teacher, washed your feet, you ought to wash one another's feet* (John 13:14).

The prophet Isaiah understood the New Covenant thousands of years ago when he wrote this:

> *He is your Teacher, and He will not continue to hide from you. You will see your Teacher with your own eyes. If you go the wrong way—to the right or to the left—you will hear a Voice behind you. It will say: "This is the right way. You should go this way"* (Isaiah 30:20-21).

I began to realize that God would not have gone to such great lengths to draw me to Himself without also giving me the power and ability to stay close to Him. He would teach me! The prophet Jeremiah saw something remarkable when he peered through the ages into our time.

> *"No one will ever teach his neighbor or relatives to know the Always-Present One. This is because **all** people will know Me—from the least important ones to the most important ones," says the Always-Present One. "I will forgive them for the evil things they did. I will forget about their sins forever"* (Jeremiah 31:34).

Now, I know what you are thinking. I struggled with the same concerns for a long, long time. Who am I supposed to believe? Should I believe what I have been taught or should I believe the Bible? At the end of the day, I have to be responsible for my own spiritual life. Look at how Paul instructed Timothy.

So, dear friends, you have always obeyed me when I was with you, but it is even more important that you obey while I am gone. Work out your own salvation with fear and trembling (Philippians 2:12).

It is not that we should not have teachers, but the teachers should guide us in our walk with God.

In this Scripture, the Lord is speaking to us through the psalmist, David:

The Always-Present One says: "I will instruct you. I will teach you which way to go. I will guide you and watch over you. So, don't be like a horse or a donkey; they don't understand. They must be led with bits, with bridles, and with reins, or they will not come near you" (Psalms 32:8-9).

The Always-Present One is my Shepherd. I have everything I need. He gives me rest in green pastures. He leads me beside calm waters (Psalms 23:1-2).

He is the One who is our instructor. Pastors and teachers lead us to the green pastures and still waters. They should keep our hearts soft and open to the Lord, so we can hear His voice and be instructed by His Spirit.

As strange and rebellious as it sounded, I began to realize that I needed to believe God rather than people. In fact, I

found this dilemma in Acts 4. Peter and John had been ar-
rested and brought to the Jerusalem Council. It was the
equivalent of the main church council. There they were ac-
cused of many things and ordered to no longer speak or
preach in the Name of Jesus. But these courageous apostles
knew their allegiance was with God first; they could not violate their conscience. They had to obey God.

> *But Peter and John answered them* [the Council],
> *"What do you think is right? What would God want?
> Should we obey you or God? We are not able to be silent.
> We must tell people about the things we saw and heard"*
> (Acts 4:19-20).

WE MUST RESPOND TO GOD

When God begins to stir your heart, you can do nothing
else but respond to Him. That was the difficult conclusion I
had come to. My heart's desire was not satisfied with the rules
and laws of mere men. I had to respond to God. It was not an
act of disobedience to humanity; it was a sovereign act of
obedience to the Lord Himself, as well as my insatiable desire
to be one with Him. I had to follow my heart.

In the last analysis, we must bear the responsibility for our
own lives. We are accountable for what we hear and for what

moves our hearts. I cannot stand before the Lord someday with the excuse that I obeyed a church rule instead of obeying the Lord, when I am certain it is the Lord. I cannot pass the responsibility for my life and the well-being of my family to another.

The apostle Paul warns us with this verse: *"I want you to understand that God is over Christ. Christ is over every male…"* (1 Cor. 11:3). There is no doubt that the floodgates of Heaven open when a believer boldly and confidently opens his or her heart to more of God's love.

I was making progress. I realized I needed to believe God first, as well as respond to Him before I responded to what others said about God. So my next questions were obvious: "What did God say about who was worthy? What did God say about who was forgiven and free from sin?" Let's look at a few of the things God says about forgiveness.

> *They said to him, "Commit yourself to the Lord Jesus and you will be saved—you and all the people living in your house"* (Acts 16:31).

> *And every person who trusts in the name of the Lord will be saved* (Acts 2:21).

Well, I certainly believed in Him, and I called upon the Name of the Lord. In fact I did it every day. I asked Jesus to forgive me all the time.

Next is a wonderful group of verses that explains the process we all go through when we ask Jesus to forgive us.

Happy is the person whose sins are forgiven.

Happy is the person whom the Always-Present One does not consider to be guilty. In that person there is nothing false.

When I kept things to myself, I felt weakness deep inside me. I moaned all day long.

Day and night, You tested me. My strength was gone, as in the summer heat....

Then I admitted my sins to You. I did not hide my guilt. I thought: "I will confess my wrongs to the Always-Present One!" And, You did forgive my sins....

For this reason, let each one who is godly pray to You while they still can. When troubles rise up like a flood of huge waters, they will not reach that person (Psalms 32:1-6).

When I repent of my sin, He forgives me. It is just that simple.

However, if we admit our sins, then God will forgive us. We can trust God; He does what is right. He will cleanse us from every evil thing (1 John 1:9).

OK, you are probably asking yourself a most important question at this point. I know because I asked the same question. What happens to me when I sin again? Notice, I did not ask what happens to me *if* I sin, but *when* I sin. If we say we have no sin after we repent, we are just lying to ourselves, to everyone around us, and to the Lord. Everyone struggles with sin. *Everyone.* We are not perfect. But if Jesus loved us, died for us, and forgave us before we ever gave our hearts to Him, how much more will He forgive us once we are serving Him and trying so hard to follow Him? He knows we are weak. He made us that way so we would understand that we cannot live the Christian life in our own strength. We need Jesus every day to strengthen us and lead us. He gives us courage to do the things we need to do.

The apostle Paul is talking directly to us when he says,

> *So, there is no condemnation now for those people who are in Christ Jesus. The law of the Spirit of life in Christ Jesus has set me free from the law of sin and death. The law was weak through human nature. God did what the law couldn't do: He sent His own Son as an offering for sin. He came with a nature like man's sinful human nature. And concerning sin, this is how God used human nature to condemn sin* (Romans 8:1-3).

We need to understand that He has forgiven us, accepted us, and made us His sons and daughters. If we can stop worrying about His ability and desire to keep forgiving us, we can concentrate on serving Him. My life has changed dramatically since I have come to understand this. Now I use my strength and anointing to serve the Lord, not to fight the guilt that Jesus has already taken away.

I am free. I have been forgiven and I am accepted. I am worthy because He has forgiven me. When I sin, I repent and keep going. I don't like the fact that I sin. Therefore, I ask God for strength to overcome sin, but I keep going forward. I keep serving in spite of myself. I know He is changing me even though sometimes it doesn't seem like it.

WHAT'S MY JOB?

You see, my job is to change the world. His ministry is to change me. I cannot change myself, but I *can* change the world. This is my success. This is what fulfills me. This is what I focus on. Now when I lay down at night, I thank God for what He helped me do that day. Sometimes the things I do are as seemingly simple as bringing smiles and hope to my family, friends, and neighbors. Whatever good I do, I do in the Name of our Lord. Of course I repent of the times I sinned, but I don't focus on them because God is working within me to change me. Because of His love and forgiveness, I am righteous. He wants me to be filled with the Holy Spirit and pray in tongues.

Listen to what Jesus says about you and the Holy Spirit.

Do any of you have a son? What would you do if your son asked you for a fish? Would any father give his son a snake? No, you would give him a fish. Or, if your son asks for an egg, would you give him a scorpion? You are evil men, yet you know how to give good gifts to your children. Surely your heavenly Father knows how to give the Holy Spirit to those people who ask Him (Luke 11:11-13).

So, who can pray in tongues? It is for everyone.

*Then Peter answered, "Change your hearts and each one of you must be immersed by the authority of Jesus the Messiah, so that your sins may be forgiven. Then you will receive the gift of the Holy Spirit. This promise is for **you** and for your children. It is also for people who are far away, for everyone whom the Lord our God may call"* (Acts 2:38-39).

The greatest adventure of life thus far is about to begin. You are soon to receive the Holy Spirit and begin to pray in tongues.

CHAPTER
5

Tongues—The Personal Prayer Language

The heavens keep telling of the glory of God. And, the skies announce what His hands have made. Day to day pours forth speech, And night to night reveals knowledge (Psalms 19:1-2).

GOD HAS A LOT TO SAY

God wants to communicate with us and through us. There is much He has to say and much He wants us to do. It is an exciting possibility to co-labor with the God of eternity.

The Lord has provided, through the blood of Jesus, many ways to pray and fellowship directly with Him. Certainly, one of the most profoundly unique ways is speaking in tongues.

There are two vital uses for speaking in tongues. The most common use is praying in tongues. We will talk about this first since it is directly related to the goal of this book.

Every believer should have a personal prayer language. This personal prayer language is a private communication language between the believer and the Lord. It can be a known tongue or an unknown tongue (further elaboration will be given regarding the differences between the two in Chapter 6). Some Scriptures even suggest that some of these unknown tongues may be the language of angels. *"Even if I speak with human languages or the language of angels, but do not have loving concern, I have only become like the noisy sound of a gong or the ringing sound from cymbals"* (1 Cor. 13:1).

Our personal prayer language is normally received when a person is baptized with the Holy Spirit. Check out these verses: *"They were all filled with the Holy Spirit and began to speak different inspired languages; the Spirit was giving them the power to do this"* (Acts 2:4).

> *Then Paul put his hands on them and the Holy Spirit came upon them. They began speaking different inspired languages and prophesying* (Acts 19:6).

When the Holy Spirit comes upon someone, it is because that person is in a place of softness and brokenness before the Lord. The heart is repentant without reservation and that person is open to all that God has for him or her. For the baptism of the Holy Spirit is the result of real desire for more of the reality of God in your life.

The baptism of the Holy Spirit is the direct response from the Lord toward a heart that is truly, deeply surrendered to Him. In spite of what difficulties are experienced afterward, that moment of surrender is marked forever by the Presence of the Lord and His personal response to you. The days, weeks, months, and years that follow will still have their troubles and will be as challenging as ever, but now you are filled with the power of God to face the most difficult of circumstances.

It is essential to realize that your prayer language is not a panacea to save you from all future trouble, but it is a tool that will help you to be victorious when you choose to use the power you have received. The key word here is *tool*. *Tongues* is not a reward for doing something good or being someone special; it is a tool that cleanses, restores, and heals the inner soul.

You should never underestimate the power released on earth when you pray in tongues. Whether the prayer is for yourself, a loved one, your friends, or your nation, the floodgates of Heaven open and God's Presence is released.

A MEMORY OF GOD'S FAITHFULNESS

Suffice it to say at this point that the initial experience will forever serve as a reminder of God's faithfulness to you. As you are painfully aware, there are times when the Presence of the Lord seems to be elusive. It is as though He is purposely staying away. God does not play that kind of hide and seek with us. He wants us; He is always there for us whether or not we know it, feel it, or understand it.

The truth is, though, if you are anything like I am, you sometimes cannot find His Presence, no matter what you do. So it is natural to either blame Him or develop some kind of a belief that allows for you not to be able to touch Him or sense His Presence. These are times when I remember what God has done for me in the past, especially when I first received my prayer language.

God does not change. His heart and desire toward us is forever sealed in Heaven. When I don't sense His Presence, I begin to pray in tongues, trusting that He is truly at work and at rest in my heart. Praying in tongues reminds me of the power and love of God in my life. It reminds me that I am in Him and He is in me, even though at times I don't feel Him. A wedding ring reminds me of Cathy's love, especially when I am traveling. I hold it in my hand and I think about her love, her laughter, and her friendship. That ring reminds me of the love of my life. It gives me great comfort.

When you pray in tongues, it will remind you of your heavenly Father's love and all He has planned for you. It always gives me great peace and reassurance when I pray in tongues. Praying in tongues will undoubtedly do the same for you.

Even though the Scriptures encourage us with many comforting passages like the words of Jesus, *"I will not abandon you, as though you were orphans. I am coming to you"* (John 14:18), and *"…I will never leave you. I will never abandon you"* (Heb. 13:5), we still have those times where we must cling to our faith without feeling anything. Those times are good since they deepen and strengthen our faith. They draw us to the realm of Spirit where God dwells and where He wants us to be always seated with Him. There, in the Spirit, we experience His manifest Presence as Paul describes in Romans 8:16: *"This same Spirit agrees with our spirits, that we are God's children."*

Paul spoke correctly and powerfully when he said, *"…the way the Spirit thinks is life and peace"* (Rom. 8:6). Our goal is to dwell in the Spirit, not just visit there. Our communion is not with the Bible as important as the Bible is; it is not with a denomination or a set of rules or even with the good things we do. Our communion is with our living Lord who dwells in the Spirit. He never goes away. He is always near to us in the Spirit. His blood has purchased for us a place with Him, and He awaits our presence with Him. Jesus came and rose from the dead so that, as He said, *"you will be where I am"* (John. 14:3).

The power of the Holy Spirit is released with great force when we pray in tongues. These prayers lift our spirit and remind us of who we really are and where we are with Him in the Spirit. The apostle Paul encouraged us to pray in tongues as a normal part of our prayer life. *"Pray with the Spirit at all times. Use all kinds of prayer and requests...."* (Eph. 6:18).

EMOTIONS ARE PART OF THE PLAN

I will make my own confession here. I have times when everything inside me struggles with the feeling that I have outlived my usefulness or that I have messed up one too many times for the Lord to still care about helping me or even hearing my prayers. These are times when I have approached the Lord with the Word and my prayer language to recover strength and hope. My favorite Scriptures in times like these are, *"Jesus Christ is the same yesterday, today, and forever"* (Heb. 13:8); *"Remember, I will always be with you even until the end of time!"* (Matt. 28:20); *"However, when the Holy Spirit comes upon you, you will receive power. You will be my witnesses in Jerusalem, in all of Judea, in Samaria, and to the farthest parts of the world"* (Acts 1:8).

Now I know as well as you do that our relationship is not completely based on feelings, but I have something very interesting for you to consider. The Scriptures compare marriage to our walk with the Lord. I can't imagine a marriage lasting without real, passionate emotion. Laughter, joy, contentment, and peace are essential to our well-being. The thought that Christians should not be emotional in their relationship with one another is unthinkable. But that is what we are told about our relationship with God. Quite frankly, that is just wrong.

My wife Cathy and I have been married for over 36 years. I can confidently tell you that we have seen and experienced the good, the bad, the ugly, and the awesome over all those years. There were times of emotional highs and emotional lows. We have experienced times of passion and times of pain. We have had times that we stayed together out of sheer grit—hanging onto the knowledge of our love and commitment together without the assistance of any positive emotion from each other or toward each other. It was during these difficult times that the memories of the good times we had together grew more important and ultimately more precious.

Yes, the emotional side of any relationship is a vital part of interacting with and loving one another. To try to remove this from our spiritual relationship with Jesus is tragic and ridiculous. We are emotional beings, made that way in His likeness and image. We serve an emotional God, who loves for us to love Him. He is not a stoic. He is not cold and impersonal. Intellectual reckoning or random duties do not determine our relationship with Him and they certainly do not fulfill the deep needs of our soul. He wants union with His people in all its emotion and beauty.

First Evidence, Lifetime Companion

Praying in tongues is usually the first evidence of being filled with the Holy Spirit. It is the initial release of His powerful Presence within us. As He pours Himself into us, the spirit within us absorbs Him like a dry sponge immersed in a pool of water. Our spirits will usually hungrily take in all they can. Our spirits' desire is now finally satisfied. The thirst is being quenched, and for the first time communion with the Lord is tangible and satisfying in a way we could never have imagined.

Throughout your life, you will find this personal prayer language will become a companion that is essential to your walk with your Lord. You will wonder how you ever survived without it. I cannot count the times that God used my prayer language to help me. When I do not know how to pray about a certain situation—which is often—I will simply pray for that issue in my prayer language. (See Romans 8:26.) Sometimes the Lord will give me some clarification, but often He will not. Nonetheless, I am comforted greatly with the knowledge that He knows the answer and that my prayer in tongues is the precise prayer that needs to be prayed.

OPEN YOUR MOUTH; HE WILL FILL IT

As Jesus fills you with His Spirit, your spiritual response will be unique, as the response is usually different in everyone. The common thread, however, is the sense of personal well-being and acceptance by the Father. It is as though we have finally surrendered everything to His will, because we have. It is a joyful sense of relief that we have finally given in to His yearning for us. We then give Him the most untamed, out-of-control part of our humanity, our tongue.

It is appropriate that the Lord require control of our most *unruly* part (see James 3:8 KJV) as we are filled with His Spirit. When we can truly lay down our gossip, slander, evil reports, and the like we can truly begin our journey of walking in the Spirit. Here is just one passage out of dozens that talk about the tongue. It is no wonder the Lord wants it tamed and submitted to Him!

The Scriptures are full of warnings about the untamed tongue. No wonder He requires its surrender to Him!

It is the same with ships. Although a ship is very large and is moved by strong winds, yet only a tiny rudder guides the ship's course, and the captain's wish controls the rudder. It is the same with our tongue. Though it may be small, it brags about great things. A big forest fire can be started by only a little flame. The tongue is like fire! Even though it is small, it can be a world of evil among other members of the body; it pollutes the entire body. It can set the whole world on fire; hell starts the fire. Mankind tames and has tamed every kind of animal in nature—beasts, birds, reptiles, and fish. However, man has not tamed the tongue; it is wild and evil, full of poison which can kill. How can we, with our tongues, praise the Lord God, our Father, and yet curse human beings who were made in the image of God? How can it be that praises and curses come from the same mouth? No, my brothers, it shouldn't be like this! (James 3:4-10).

OK, I am sure you are getting the idea here. When we are filled with the Spirit, we are asked to offer our tongue to the Lord, a fitting tribute to how the Lord will change our speech to glorify Him in all we do. Not only do we speak in an unknown tongue, we also notice that our native language changes. No longer do we want to use our tongue for evil; but we will find that we want to sanctify it, that is, we want to preserve our tongue for words that encourage, bless, love, and heal.

PRAY IN TONGUES

When we pray in tongues, we bypass the human will and human desires. Thus we bypass the very human resistance that normally accompanies the thought of doing something we don't want to do. You see the Holy Spirit searches out the needs of the heart and prays for us in tongues. He does not ask our permission. We have already given Him permission when we gave our tongue to Him. Now He is free to work in us, through us, and among us. We have given the Lord free reign.

We think we are so certain about how God should answer our prayers. We spend most of our prayer time counseling Him on how He should take care of a situation; but He knows best. When we release our prayer tongue to Him, we begin to see answers that we could never have imagined. Things change so much; it is like we are watching our own lives on a stage. I have been praying in tongues for 36 years and I am still amazed at how it works. If there is one confession I can truly make, it is this: He knows better than I do. His ways are higher and better than mine. I love to see Him intervene in my life and in the lives of those I love.

By going before the Lord in tongues, we are offering our-selves to the Lord in the most complete way we can. It is as though we are saying to the Lord, "I have no idea what the so-lution is in this situation. But I trust You. I trust the Holy Spirit will search out the thoughts and intents of all those involved. I believe that He will offer the prayer that is exactly the right prayer for this moment. Although I do not know what is being prayed, I trust that it is Your best will for this situation."

This Scripture is the best description of the function of praying in tongues:

> *We don't know how we should pray, but the Spirit helps our weakness. He personally talks to God for us with feel-ings which our language cannot express. God searches all men's hearts. He knows what the Spirit is thinking. The Spirit talks to God in behalf of holy people, using the manner which pleases God. We know that all things work together for good for people who love God. They are called for God's purpose* (Romans 8:26-28).

HE TEACHES US TO PRAY

It is OK when we just don't know how to pray. Some-times He will show us what we are praying for as we pray in tongues. I often find that my faith is built and I can believe for hard things, like praying for a mountain to move. That is because I can sense what the prayer is for; and so it builds my faith to know that God told me what the real need is and that the Holy Spirit is praying for it as well.

I once had a friend with whom I prayed very often. He was single. Not only that but he was convinced that God had told him he would never marry but would live his life solely devoted to the Lord. I had a hard time seeing that in him, but I am not his judge. One sunny afternoon we were sitting on the deck behind his house. We talked and prayed over many things, most of which I will never remember. But there was *one* prayer that I will never forget. It changed His life and changed my perspective of the power of praying in tongues.

He began to pray in English, "Lord Jesus, I thank You that you have called me to be a eunuch in the house of the Lord. Thank You that You have called me to dedicate my life to You in service. I give myself to You and I want to express my contentment with this calling."

"OK," I thought, "fair enough." But then he started to pray in tongues and I heard a remarkable thing. In my heart, I heard the real prayer of his spirit within him. "Lord, I need a *woman!* I want to get married and have kids and a family. I don't like being single. Please help me find a woman!" Needless to say I was shocked, but I had to hide my laughter. I knew it was God. It was the last thing I ever expected to hear. I do not believe that God is a busybody, but I do think He wanted me to know my friend so I could pray with him. Needless to say, it wasn't long before he was dating, then engaged, married with a home and a house full of sons. Incredible. Wonderful. Thank God that He prays for us and through us so that the true desires of hearts can be fulfilled!

Tongues can also give us focus when there really needs to be focus and none seems to be available. I know many, many instances where a believer began praying in tongues in the moment of crisis and unexpected turmoil. I have called upon the Lord during many immediate crises, including skidding on a snowy road, receiving a difficult phone call, and my sons' first time out with the family car!

But this kind of praying in tongues and praying with real understanding was a regular occurrence for the apostle Paul, who said this about praying in tongues: *"So, what should I do? I will pray with my spirit and pray with understanding, too. I will sing to God with my spirit and sing with understanding, too"* (1 Cor. 14:15).

Paul also said this about his own experience with tongues: *"I thank God that I speak in inspired languages more than all of you"* (1 Cor. 14:18). If the apostle Paul thought he needed to speak in tongues, I am sure I need to as well! When we pray in tongues, we encourage and build up our own spirit: *"The one who is speaking an inspired language is only helping himself…"* (1 Cor. 14:4).

WE NEED HELP

I don't think that I am the only one who tries to think through problems. I don't think I am the only one who tries to determine what others need according to my own logical way of thinking. But when I do try to determine how to pray, and I am sometimes wrong in my determination, I end up just polluting the spiritual atmosphere with fleshy words based on finite ability to discern the things of the spirit realm. The five senses will never understand the Spirit. The mind of a million people is still foolishness to God. He can see, hear, and understand in every realm, while we are largely limited to the realms that are examined by the five senses.

No wonder the Scriptures say that *"God's 'nonsense' is still wiser than the 'wisdom' of human beings"* (1 Cor. 1:25). It is imperative that we allow the Lord, who sees all, hears all, and understands all things, to have His way when we pray. It is the fastest, most direct route to the will of God. Let's pray His will. When we don't know His will, pray in tongues!

GENUINE RELATIONSHIP

When I talk about a relationship with God, this is the kind of relationship I am pointing to. He wants genuine, soft-hearted people through whom He can and will show His glory. A relationship with God is not a one-time prayer. It is not a membership in a church or perfect attendance in Sunday school. It is a daily interactive fellowship with God. This relationship involves an awareness of His Presence and an expectation that He can and will intervene and interact with you at any time of the day or night.

PRAYER LANGUAGE IS WORSHIP

Your prayer language is an integral part of this relationship with your Lord. Your prayer language is worship. It is a language that speaks heavenly *sweet nothings* to your Lord and Father. It worships and extols the Lord, lifting your heart to Him and your spirit to the heights of all God has for you. Your prayer language understands how you feel about the Lord and worships Him with words that best describe how you feel.

There are times when my heart is full of such love for my wife Cathy that I cannot find adequate words to express to her how I feel. So I have to be satisfied with fumbling for words that often don't make sense to her! But, thank God, she understands and accepts my meager attempts at some romantic conversation, as she knows I intend it to be loving and comforting.

PRAYER LANGUAGE IS INVITATIONAL

The Holy Spirit will often move in your spirit, urging you to pray in tongues. It is an awesome experience and is a normal part of your walk with God. It is just incredible that the Lord will determine that He wants you to pray and then purposely move inside, stirring your heart to respond to Him. What a compliment to have your Lord look at you and say, "I want My friend to pray right now," and then purposefully move in your heart to that end. Sometimes you will never know what you are praying for. Sometimes you will have a sense of worship or enveloping glory as you pray in your private language.

I often compare this experience to sitting with Cathy while reading or resting. Nothing really is said or needs to be said. Just being together is fulfilling and exciting. God has wanted fellowship with His people from the beginning of time. Although He is a giver, He wants fellowship. He wants us to be near Him and enjoy His Presence. Enjoying Him just because He is God without the pretext of needing something or wanting something is one of the most powerful experiences you can have with Him.

Have you ever had someone approach you, giving you compliments or telling you how much they love you? I bet that more than once when this happened, you wondered what this person really wanted. Cathy and I have raised five sons and we know that tactic well. It was never that we did not want to help our sons with whatever we could, but we did not like them to "use" the words of *love* and *concern* as a way to get something. There is a time for loving exchanges of words and there is the time for simply asking for what we need. We tend to think that we have to worship to get something from God or praise to get His attention so that we can ask for something.

God wants and enjoys times of just being together without using those tender times of His nearness to ask Him for something. If we are secure in our friendship with the Lord, we will soon come to know that this kind of thinking is both unnecessary and non-relational. There are times and purposes for all things in our walk with God. Your prayer language is often just worship to Him. We need to relax and enjoy His Presence simply for the sake of His Presence.

OUR PRAYER LANGUAGE GETS THINGS DONE

On a recent trip to Italy, I closed the Sunday morning meeting with an invitation to pray for folks, as I usually do.

On this particular morning, I was surprised when a teenage girl dressed in Goth came forward for prayer. She waited patiently as I prayed for others ahead of her. I looked at her again and again, trying to get a sense of her deepest need. I was not sure if she had come by choice or by decree, but she was there nonetheless.

Her lips, tongue, nose, ears, and eyebrows were pierced, and she wore typical Goth jewelry in every piercing. She showed no emotion as she waited for me. When I finally approached her, she simply closed her eyes without a gesture of any kind. I took her hands into mine and began waiting for the Lord to tell me something, but I did not have an idea about how to proceed. I finally decided to simply pray for her in tongues knowing that whatever the need, the Holy Spirit would find it out and pray for her through me.

I could sense the Holy Spirit probing her spirit when suddenly she began to weep. I continued praying, realizing that the Lord had landed on an important issue in her life. Unfortunately for me, I had no idea what it was. Several minutes passed and the urge to pray only grew stronger. I had learned long ago not to rush to the work of the Spirit. If it took longer than expected, then the others would just have to wait. I cannot stop until I feel in my heart that the prayer is over. By now the girl's parents were with her, also praying quietly. I could see the hope and the urgency in their eyes. Their love for her was strong. I knew this day would be a turning point in her life.

As my prayer in tongues for her grew in intensity, her tears grew more uncontrollable. I knew God was doing something for her, moving a mountain that only she knew existed. After 20 minutes or so, the prayer subsided. I had a release from the Lord, but I did not know what, if anything, had happened. The only thing I knew for certain was that the prayer was intense and landed on a place in her that was most desperate. As she continued to sob, her parents took her back to her seat. I could see the disappointment in their eyes. All I could do was trust the Lord that His will was done.

Some may ask why I did not pray for her so she could understand me. Some would wonder why I did not cast out a devil or give her a verse from the Bible. My goal, however, when I pray for someone is to be as true to the moving of the Holy Spirit within as I can possibly be. I don't want to say something that God is not saying. I don't want to make something up to make anyone feel better. The worst thing you can do for someone is misrepresent the Lord. It is bad for them and for the work of the Lord in their lives. It is also bad for me. If I minister in a way that is not consistent with what God is saying, how will He trust me in the future to reach one of His own?

The meeting ended, and the afternoon was full of conversation about the morning service and this young teen in particular. The conclusion was as it always is: Trust the Holy Spirit and His work in the hearts of His people.

That evening the service was in the same church as the morning service. People gathered and all was as it should be. I again closed the meeting with a call to prayer.

I began praying for a young teen. She had a beautiful smile and a look of utter contentment. Suddenly Pastor Pietro interrupted me with a shocked look on his face. "Pastor Don, do you recognize this girl?" I looked at her closely, but was certain I had never seen her. "No, I never saw her before in my life." When Pastor Pietro translated my response to the church, everyone laughed and began to praise the Lord. The young girl looked at me and said, "God moved a mountain for me this morning when you prayed for me." I was shocked with disbelief! How could this be that Goth girl I had prayed for in the morning? She was completely changed. The facial jewelry was gone, her color was changed, and her clothes were completely different. Her parents wept with joy, and we all paused to thank God for His miracle-working power.

Our prayer language moves mountains. The Holy Spirit searches the heart of the person we are praying for and prays exactly what is needed. It is amazing, powerful, and life-changing. We do not need to know what is going on either in our hearts or the ones for whom we pray. In God's time it always comes out. In the meantime, let God be God; He does not need our counsel, advice, or help.

TRUSTING THE HOLY SPIRIT

The most wonderful place anyone can come to in his or her walk with the Lord is to learn to trust the work of the Holy Spirit in the hearts of others. It is human nature to want to have a part in everything we see God doing. Certainly we do have a part, but we must learn to let God do His part while we do ours. For our part, God uses our faith to believe what we are praying for. He uses our hands to impart His Presence. He uses our smiles to impart comfort and confidence. He uses our bodies to carry His Presence to the four corners of the earth. When these things are in place, we simply need to yield to the flow of the Holy Spirit within and trust that He is doing what needs to be done.

> We don't know how we should pray, but the Spirit helps our weakness. He personally talks to God for us with feelings which our language cannot express. God searches all men's hearts. He knows what the Spirit is thinking. The Spirit talks to God in behalf of holy people, using the manner which pleases God (Romans 8:26-27).

CHAPTER
6

Tongues—the Gift

So, my brothers, eagerly desire the ability to prophesy. And, don't try to stop people from speaking in inspired languages (1 Corinthians 14:39).

L et's be careful not to confuse the two purposes of tongues. They are very different. Just like there are different kinds of music, dance, food, and so on, there are different kinds of tongues, each with a distinct purpose.

The Gift and the Prayer Language

I will not go into great detail here because this is not the purpose of the book. I do, however, want to be sure that you understand that your prayer language, praying in tongues, is your personal "hotline" to the Lord. The *gift* of speaking in tongues, on the other hand, serves a completely different purpose and is used primarily in a setting where the gift of tongues and one or more of the accompanying gifts are present in a gathering of believers.

You will sometimes know what you are praying for when you pray in tongues. As you learn to be attentive to the Holy Spirit, He will often allow you to see the need and even gain insight into the situation you are praying for. This is a normal experience to have when you pray in the Spirit.

When you are baptized with the Holy Spirit, you receive your personal prayer language which, by the way, can change as the Holy Spirit moves within your heart. You will have the urge to pray in tongues often throughout the day. When this happens to me and I am alone, I will pray aloud. But if I am around others, I will pray in tongues silently, since it is a personal communication between my Lord and me.

Often the urge or prompting to pray in tongues will come while I am with someone. The Lord may want me to pay special attention to the conversation and to His leading within my heart. The Holy Spirit often alerts me that there is a special need that I can address with the person I am with or that He just wants me to pray for that individual. The secret is not to rush into anything until I am sure of the leading of the Lord.

Worship will also cause the Holy Spirit to arise in you in a mighty way. Whether you are alone or in a gathering of believers, your personal prayer language will often arise within and beg expression. When the prompting to pray in tongues comes in a gathering, it is important for you to understand the people you are with. Although your personal prayer language does not need to be interpreted when you pray in tongues in a gathering, it will cause a problem if it is not taught or understood among the people you are with.

WHEN TO FOLLOW

My personal rule is to follow what is happening among the other people. If there are people praying in tongues quietly, then I know I can as well. If there are many people worshiping and singing in tongues, I know it is accepted and so I will be free to do likewise. But if it is not evident among the people, then I will refrain, as I will not want to cause someone to stumble over my liberty in Christ. (See

First Corinthians 8:9.) Freedom to respond to the Holy Spirit is an awesome thing to have. But it is also an awesome responsibility. Although it is true that most of the confusion comes from either the lack of teaching or incorrect teaching, you never have the right to impose your experience on another. Remember that God did not violate your will, but waited for you to have an open heart. You must also respect other believers' journeys. So if you have doubt, don't do it. People will know there is something different about you by the fruit of love, compassion, mercy, kindness, and the other fruit of God's Presence in your life.

Now, let's move on. Just because you have a personal prayer language, does not necessarily mean you will have the *gift* of speaking in tongues. When the *gift* of tongues is exercised, it is when the church is basically quiet or at the end of song. It is spoken loudly for all to clearly hear. Then the congregation will wait until someone speaks with the interpretation. It is a mistake to think that a prayer tongue needs to be interpreted. But it is also a mistake to pray in tongues so loud that the congregation thinks it is a message from God in tongues. It is best to pray quietly enough so that it is only heard by those close to you. If the church has been properly taught, the congregation will easily understand the difference between a prayer language and the message in tongues.

If the Lord uses you to speak a message in tongues, it is quite often the same language you have become accustomed to using. In many instances, God will give a fresh language, and sometimes you will speak a known language fluently. It is important that you know it can happen any way the Lord wants it to happen. Your job is to simply flow with the Holy Spirit and respond in simple love, faith, and devotion to your Lord. Not everything can be categorized and marked on a chart. God is still God and He will do whatever He wants to do, even if we do not understand it.

WHEN TO SPEAK

The gift of speaking in tongues is certainly a special manifestation of the Holy Spirit. It is designed to get either our attention or the attention of a non-believer. It is a sign that God wants to speak to us, show us something we need to be aware of, or draw us closer to Him.

You may wonder how hearing someone with the gift of speaking in tongues will help us to hear the Lord or understand anything. After all, it is in an unknown tongue! The answer is simple: when someone speaks with the gift of tongues, there should always be an interpretation of the unknown language into the language that is understood by those in the meeting. So God gets our attention with the miracle of an unknown tongue when it is spoken in a meeting. Then someone else that understands the meaning of the unknown tongue will give its meaning for all to be taught and encouraged. Often when there is no one present to interpret the message in the unknown tongue, the one who spoke in the unknown tongue may be given the interpretation. But this does not always happen.

Since the gift of tongues is used in a public setting, as a focal part of a meeting and since that message needs to be interpreted, someone with either the gift of interpretation or someone who can interpret should be present. It is a misnomer that only someone with the gift of interpretation can interpret the message in tongues. God can and will use anyone with an open heart who is attentive to the Spirit of God. He will even use the same person who spoke the message in tongues to interpret.

There are several things that will sometimes cause a message in tongues to go uninterpreted. Often, it is not the fault of the person who spoke in tongues, but of those who could have interpreted the message, but didn't.

We need to understand that it takes a bit of faith to speak up when you are the one with the interpretation. Often the person who is supposed to give the interpretation does not have the confidence to speak at that moment. There may be distracting issues that prevent one person from acting on what God is showing. Therefore, the Holy Spirit will go to another person with the interpretation. The Holy Spirit may give several people the opportunity to speak from the same message in tongues, thus confirming the word of the Lord. *"The testimony of two or three people is true"* (2 Cor. 13:1). That is why it is important to give time to this process. We are imperfect vessels carrying the anointing. The human element within will often cause us to resist the urging of the Holy Spirit.

Nonetheless, if there is a message in tongues and there is no one to interpret, the world will not come to an end and neither does the Kingdom of God hang in the balance. The meeting simply proceeds and the one who spoke the message in tongues will need to be more careful to be sure God is moving through him or her before speaking.

A congregation that is taught the mysteries of the Spirit will understand the dynamics of the event and will not be confused. Confusion only comes when mixed signals are sent from the leadership or no teaching occurs on the topic of the gifts of the Spirit.

These Scriptures offer the foundation for the working of the gifts of the Spirit in a gathering of believers:

> *The showing of the Spirit is given to each one for the good of everyone: the ability to speak wisely is given*

through the Spirit to one person. The ability to give knowl-edge is given by the same Spirit to another person. A differ-ent person receives faith by the same Spirit. The ability to heal diseases is given to another by the one Spirit. The ability to work miracles is given to someone else. The abil-ity to prophesy is given to another person. The ability to see the difference between what spirits teach is given to another one. The ability to speak different inspired languages is given to one. The ability to interpret inspired languages is given to someone else. All of these powers are given by one and the same Spirit. He distributes them to each person as He chooses (1 Corinthians 12:7-11).

Now, brothers, if I come speaking inspired languages to you, what good will you get out of it? I may speak to you by revelation, inspired knowledge, prophecy, or in-spired teaching. Lifeless instruments, such as a flute or a harp, produce a sound. This sound must be made clearly or no one can recognize the tune which is being played on the flute or the harp. If the bugle makes a sound which is not clear, no one will prepare for battle (1 Corinthians 14:6-8).

Again, the lack of an interpretation of an unknown tongue when spoken as a focal part of the meeting is neither positive or negative for the service. It is a training and instructional opportunity for the entire church to learn and be freed to flow in the Spirit. An environment of security, acceptance, patience and love will, in time, produce the desired results.

MIRACULOUS USE OF TONGUES

On the Day of Pentecost, just after Jesus was raised from the dead, the disciples and many others were together as the Lord commanded them. As you know, this was when the Holy Spirit was poured out and believers first began to speak in other tongues. Can you imagine the strangeness of the setting? Can you imagine that there was no warning, no prophecy, no real preparation for what was happening to them? They only knew to get together and wait for the *promise of the Father* as Jesus had instructed them. *"Listen, I am sending My Father's promise upon you, but you must stay in Jerusalem until you are clothed with that power from heaven"* (Luke 24:49). Even though they had no idea what the promise was or how they would receive it, they obediently gathered and waited. I guess that all that time with the Lord helped them to expect the unexpected and to open their hearts in an out-of-the-box fashion. That is the only way they could have received a spiritual gift without the scriptural clarity.

When the house in which the disciples were gathered began to shake and the tongues of fire began to appear, they also began to have the strange urge to speak with words they did not understand (see Acts 2:1-4). It would have been something incredible to watch as these faithful believers opened their hearts to something they had never before heard. That first Pentecost was a faith-building power surge that affected them and all those around them for the rest of their lives. In fact, this book you are reading is a testimony to the power that was unleashed on that day, more than 2,000 years ago. It turned into an evangelistic event born in the heart of God for that time and for all time. Now you, as well, are about to become part of the great outpouring that the apostles and other disciples experienced. Here is part of the account of that event as it is recorded in the Acts of the Apostles:

> *They were all filled with the Holy Spirit and they began to speak different inspired languages; the Spirit was giving them the power to do this. There were some devout Jewish men staying in Jerusalem at this time. These men were from every country in the world. A large group of them came together because they heard the noise. They were confused. The apostles were speaking and every man heard in his own language. The Jewish people were all amazed at this. They didn't understand how the apostles could do this. They said, "Look! These men whom we hear speaking are all from Galilee! But each of us is hearing them in our own native language. We*

are: Parthians, Medes, Elamites, those living in Mesopotamia, from Judea, from Cappadocia, from Pontus, from Asia, from Phrygia, from Pamphylia, from Egypt, from parts of Libya around Cyrene, visitors from Rome, Cretans, Arabians. Some of us were born Jews. Others are converts to Judaism. We can hear these men in our own languages! We can all understand the wonderful things they are saying about God (Acts 2:4-11).

More than 3,000 people gave their hearts to the Lord that wonderful day. It was certainly something that none of the disciples and apostles could have ever imagined. Had you asked them what God was about to do, I am certain that none of them would have guessed correctly!

STAY OPEN, STAY SOFT

God still uses tongues in powerful and unusual ways today. It is important that we do not limit God in what He can do and will do. Just because something is not our experience does not mean we should resist it. We must grow daily in our desire to wrap our faith around a God who is eternally huge and all-powerful. He is bigger than our finite minds and cannot be put in a box of doctrine, denomination, or doubt. He will always do things bigger than we can imagine or think.

Glory to God! He is able to do so much more than we can even think of or ask for. God uses the power that is working in us. Glory to God among all the people He has called out and in Christ Jesus for all generations forever and ever. Amen (Ephesians 3:20-21).

When Cathy and I were first married, we were both students at Shippensburg University. One evening we decided to drive to an area called Big Flat located at the top of South Mountain about ten miles away. We often went there to pray, as it was quiet and the night sky was so beautiful. There were ten to fifteen of us there that night, along with a young Jewish man who was a friend to several of us. As we began to pray, the Holy Spirit moved among us, as was normal at our prayer meetings. Most were praying in tongues when this Jewish man fell to his knees and called out to Jesus to forgive him. We were quite shocked as we did not know what had happened to him.

After he recovered from his experienced, he told us that he heard someone praying and worshiping in fluent Hebrew. The words spoken praised the Lord and talked of the Savior, Jesus Christ. Many other students came to the Lord as a result of this one event.

God will often show Himself with the miraculous where His people are open to Him. The key is to understand that

God is bigger than our understanding. He is bigger than our opinions. His ways are far more moving than our ways. If we will but wait for Him with faith and childlike anticipation, we will see and experience incredible things.

A pastor who allows the free moving of the Holy Spirit understands that with time, proper training, and instruction, a regular flow of all the gifts of the Spirit will be a powerful addition and encouragement to the local Body of Christ. We must remember that God never instituted lifeless rituals or meaningless activity for His people to perform. Everything we do is intended to be a result of true life or to bring true life. The gifts of the Spirit, of which speaking in tongues is one, need to be embraced as the tools of growth and encouragement that God intended them to be.

When I was a young boy, my twin brother Ron and I worked closely with our father in the family business. The small fleet of vehicles that my dad owned often needed to be serviced. My dad seldom took them to a garage to be repaired, opting to do most of the work himself. That meant that Ron and I learned a lot about the tools of car repair. I remember the first time I tried to use a socket wrench. My dad was working on one car and he asked me to take off the oil filter of another vehicle that needed replacing.

By the time my dad realized what I was doing, I had nearly broken his old wrench. I had already completely destroyed the old oil filter that was still tightly attached to the car. He was not happy, but he did not forbid me from using the wrench again. He simply began, once again, to instruct me on how to properly use the wrench. I was not afraid of trying it again, nor was I ashamed for messing up the oil filter. Embarrassed, yes, but more determined than ever to get it right the next time.

In the same way, misuse of the gifts of the Spirit is a poor reason not to allow them. If patient instruction, gentle correction, and plenty of encouraging love are used, a congregation will emerge as a vibrant center of the supernatural activity of the Lord. Such supernatural contact is not only desired, it is essential for victory in today's world.

> *So, my brothers, eagerly desire the ability to prophesy. And, don't try to stop people from speaking in inspired languages* (1 Corinthians 14:39).

THE GREATEST IS LOVE

But like Paul, I will tell you there is a greater way. That greater way is to simply love the Lord, love those around you, and allow that love to flow through you. With the sincerity of your heart intact, the Lord will have His way in everything. Responding to love is always the best plan to win the world for Jesus. The main goal is not to get everything right; it is to get everyone loved. Don't be afraid to be who you are and who you are becoming in Him.

> *…Even if I speak with human languages or the language of angels, but do not have loving concern, I have only become like the noisy sound of a gong or the ringing sound from cymbals. I may have the ability to prophesy, know all secrets, possess all knowledge, and have the kind of faith which can move mountains, but if I don't have concern for others, I am nothing* (1 Corinthians 13:1-2).

Understanding that Jesus wants to live His life through you is the greatest encouragement, the greatest compliment, and the greatest hope that any of us have! It is not hard to follow the Lord. Your faith, your desire, and your hunger will lead you into all He has for you. Do not be afraid.

> *Now these three things last: faith, hope, and love—but the most important of these is love* (1 Corinthians 13:13).

CHAPTER 7

Prayer Language for Children

*Then Peter answered, "Change your hearts and each one of you must be immersed by the authority of Jesus the Messiah, so that your sins may be forgiven. Then you will receive the gift of the Holy Spirit. This promise is for **you** and for your children. It is also for people who are far away, for everyone whom the Lord our God may call" (Acts 2:38-39).*

T here has never been a God-imposed ending or age requirement to receive the baptism of the Holy Spirit and your personal prayer language. Peter had an important revelation about the plan of God, and he was quick to share that truth with all who were listening to him during that first Pentecost and with all of us as well. When Peter spoke the words quoted above, he saw, by the Spirit, through time and space into eternity. He saw the ages unfolding before him and the promises of God filling and overflowing every generation to come. Peter declared with pinpoint prophetic accuracy that the burden of the Lord was for all peoples and for all time.

We must understand that restrictions and limitations to God's work are usually either self-imposed or placed on us by others. Whatever the reasons, they are not important now. What is important is that God pours out His Spirit upon all who are open to Him. This includes children.

Understanding the desire of the Lord Jesus toward children will help you answer questions that are on the minds of many believers. When are children old enough to receive the Holy Spirit? Do they have to understand what is happening to them? Is it possible for them to experience the gifts of the Spirit at a very young age?

EQUIPPING THE CHILDREN

Cathy and I have five sons so this was a question we grappled with early in our marriage and ministry. We wanted our sons to be properly equipped so they could face and be victorious over all the temptations of school and the media. We knew we could not always be with them, looking over their shoulders to guide them. But there was One sent by Jesus who would be with them to guide, instruct, and protect. That Person is the Holy Spirit.

As Cathy and I looked at their future, we understood the struggles they would face. We were painfully aware of what we struggled with as teens, and we knew things had only gotten much worse over the years. We knew that God's power within them was their best hope of a successful journey through high school and university. They needed what we had, and they needed it much earlier than we received it if the Holy Spirit was to benefit them when they needed Him the most. But we didn't want them to just survive their teen years. We wanted them to have success and fun. We wanted them to win where we did not. Our prayer was, and still is today, that their Lord would lead them to greater places than Cathy and I could only imagine.

Children should always go further in their faith and in their profession than their parents. The two cannot be separated. When we respond to God, yielding to Him in everything, He opens doors for us and grants us favor in every area of life. My father established three businesses in his lifetime. He was a hard-working man who focused on his family and their needs. As he taught us how to work with him, Dad would often tell us, "You will do better than I have done. I didn't learn this stuff about business until I was 40 years old. You are learning these lessons at a much younger age!" I clearly remember my father saying, "I am doing all I can to help you. When I am old and gray, I will be proud to see how much more you have accomplished than I did." My dad did not live long enough to see the success of his sons, but he lives on in us and we work hard to "make him proud."

He was also a man of faith. He believed the Lord and served Him as best he could. The strong foundation of family love and family beliefs were written on our hearts by the loving example of my mom and dad.

In many ways we picked up where my parents left off. We did not have to re-learn many of the same lessons they suffered throughout their lives because we learned them from their experience. However, to be perfectly honest, we made our share of bone-headed mistakes. But hopefully, we will be able to transfer these lessons to our children so they won't have to go through all we had to experience.

JUST PLOW THE FIELD ONCE

Our children should not have to clear the same land and plow the same fields that we did. We need to plow and plant so they can reap a harvest from our labor and go on to bigger fields! We must broaden our vision of what the Kingdom of God is and of how our children can expand the Kingdom here on earth. I often say to my sons, "I didn't find the Lord until I was 20, and I didn't have my head screwed on right until much later." (And some people still wonder about me.) "But now look at you; you were filled with the Holy Spirit and you were praying in tongues when you were three and four years old! You are hearing God and responding to Him at such a young age. Just think how much more you are going to do for the Kingdom than I have done!"

What would our children accomplish if we would train them, point them toward the Lord Jesus, and tell them that God expects them to do better and to go farther than we have? With God's help, our sons and daughters will achieve much more than we could possibly hope, dream, or imagine. Our children will take the torch and live with a greater sense of His Presence, a deeper awareness of His power.

The beginning of this is living a genuine believer's life before them and presenting to them the same opportunities we have had ourselves and that we offer others. It means we allow them to dream and imagine even the wildest imaginations. It is our own self-imposed limitations that have prevented us from doing all we could do. If we are not careful, we pass the same limitations onto our kids.

Better at Praying in Tongues Than English

That is why when our son Donald came us to about a vision he had, we were quick to listen and also to encourage. Early one Sunday morning while we were driving to the morning service, Donald began to tell us what had happened to him. He had just turned four years old when he told us about his amazing encounter with the Lord.

"I was sleeping and I felt someone shaking me awake. When I opened my eyes, Jesus was standing next to my bed. He was smiling at me. Jesus said He wanted to live in my heart and asked me if He could come in. He said He would be good to me and He would be my friend." Donald told the story with little emotion, as though this was a normal thing to happen. Donald told the Lord that He wanted Jesus to live inside Him. "Then He just disappeared, and I knew He was in my heart."

Cathy and I were so excited. This was a great event for him and for us all. But the pastor in me immediately began to think of what I should do next. "Donnie, this is so great! Your mom and I are so proud of you!" We encouraged him to talk to Jesus and listen to His voice. I added, "Donnie, next you will receive the Holy Spirit and you will be able to pray in tongues just like Mommy and Daddy."

Donald shook his head and responded, "Oh, I already do that. Jesus told me He wanted me to start to pray in the angels' words like you and Mommy do. So I started to pray that way."

"What?" I asked him, more than a little shocked. Cathy turned around to look at him in the back seat of the car. "You already speak in tongues?"

With a bit if an indignant smile, he responded, "I do it all the time." I thought Cathy was going to jump out of her seat.

"Can you do it now? I would love to hear you pray in tongues." Without a second of hesitation, Donnie began to pray in a wonderful, flowing heavenly language. It sent chills up our spines to realize that God will fill anyone who is open-hearted and soft, even a small child. My goodness…he was speaking in tongues better than he spoke English at the time!

In Donald's tiny world, he had met a great big God who had blessed him and filled him with the Holy Spirit, including his very own prayer language. In the years to come, we would realize what an important event that was—not just for Donald but for Cathy and me as well. Our ministry to our children and to the children in the church we pastored dramatically changed as we realized that even the youngest among us could and should experience the fullness of the Holy Spirit and the power of praying in tongues.

UNEXPECTED SURPRISE

The Lord did something very awesome for our family when our children were young. He brought Dian Layton into our lives. She has an awesome understanding of the powerful, faith-packed spirit within children. Although we had experienced two of our sons sovereignly filled with the Holy Spirit, she brought us to the realization as well as the understanding that our children could go further in God than we could possibly imagine.

Dian, her husband Barry, along with their two sons Ben and John (the boys n' Barry), are an exceptional example of what a family can be when surrendered to the Lord without the restrictions of limited thinking. Our children grew up together for many years. We watched their spirits develop as they grew in the Lord.

Dian has taught me much over the years. She never ceases to amaze me with her simple faith, not only in the Lord Jesus but the children she ministers to. I have watched her as she prayed for auditoriums full of children. I witnessed these children being filled with the Holy Spirit and praying in tongues. They wept before the Lord as He filled them with hope, power, and destiny. It has been such a moving experience to see so many children weeping for joy and quietly praying in their newly given language. I found myself close to jealousy as

I watched, time and time again, the same things happening to so many children. "Lord, I want that. Why did I have to miss getting this [and instead receive it so much later]? I want what they have!"

OK, you are already anticipating what happened. I felt a verse rising slowly but powerfully from the depths of my heart. The words of Jesus ignited my faith as they echoed through my soul and said, *"I am telling you the truth: If you don't change and become like little children, you will never enter the kingdom of heaven. The person who humbles himself like this little child is the most important one in the kingdom of heaven. The person who, in My name, welcomes a little child such as this one welcomes Me"* (Matt. 18:3-5).

If you are like most adults, it is not common to think that God can do much with children until they are at least close to their teen years. We basically babysit the kids with repetitive Bible stories, arts, and crafts. Then we wonder why they grow up with such a cynical view of church. To them, Sunday mornings are boring and wearisome. But there is a secret that is beginning to get out. Dian has dedicated her life to getting this word to the nations. The spirit of a child is the same as the spirit of an adult. It needs to be fed, nurtured, strengthened, and challenged. Children can and should be filled with the Holy Spirit. They can and should pray in tongues. They can and should be taught faith to move mountains.

Children can hear God's voice and experience remarkable miracles. Their spiritual prayer language can be the Christ-centered foundation that keeps them connected to their Lord, as they navigate through the difficult teenage years. Now more than ever, children need the early start of being connected to their Lord, knowing He loves them, forgives them, understands them, and will never ever leave them alone.

This is the powerful generation of children who will change the world because we won't tell them that they can't! The supernatural will propel them into the exciting and fulfilling reality of Christ and lead them to great success as they respond to Him and His plan for them. For most of us, it is an enviable thought that children can have such an incredible head start in their walk with the Lord. Let us open our own hearts and allow the Lord to change our minds so He might move among the children within our areas of influence.

The hearts of children are open, innocent, and vulnerable. Just as baby sparrows open their mouths and close their eyes waiting for food, children are open and ready to receive anyone who happens to walk by with a worm in the mouth. God has already prepared children's hearts; they are open to receive without debate and with far less instruction than most of us were. Don't be afraid. The Holy Spirit and praying in tongues are not just for adults; they are for all who come to Him with childlike faith and an open heart.

Can you imagine how much easier school would be if our children knew and experienced the power needed for living? Can you imagine the moral anchor that genuine relationship would bring? God would spare children the pain and anguish of their teenage years. He would comfort them and strengthen them in their battle against temptation. He would be near them to protect, lead, and teach. You cannot always be with your children, but the Holy Spirit can be and He will.

CHAPTER
8

First Things First

JESUS IS LORD

Our spiritual journey started long before we were ever born. In fact, it began before time began when our Father in Heaven determined to have a people with whom He could enjoy conversation and friendship. Contrary to popular belief, God's plan for humanity was not just to populate Heaven. He wanted people who would love Him and walk with Him because they chose to do so, right here on earth.

Therefore, long before time began, God saw us in His Spirit and began the chain of events that in time resulted in all of us being here. The hunger and desire you have for Him were given to you by the Lord. The Lord also gave me the hunger that I have in my heart. These events have brought us to this place in time where our paths have crossed and you are reading this book.

His goal is to have people who not only love Him, but who also enjoy being with Him now, on this side of eternity, in this dimension of time and space. His love for us and His desire for fellowship with us were the motivations in sending His Son Jesus to earth in order to cleanse us from our sin. Jesus' death and resurrection also broke the power of sin, the human will, and the enemy of our soul— the devil.

The Scriptures make it clear that Jesus is the foundation of our freedom from sin. He is why we can be forgiven and He is the reason we can enjoy daily, interactive friendship with God. Jesus is the Doorway to everything godly and every good thing in Heaven.

The doorway into His Presence is wide open. Now men and women can decide for themselves, individually, if they will follow Jesus; but there are no *shotgun weddings* in the Spirit. We must come to Him voluntarily. We must understand that we are sinners in need of a Savior. We need help, guidance, and strength from the One who sees and has a plan for us. We need a Lord. We need Jesus. Only when this is clear to us can we start on this journey of discovery with our Lord Jesus.

There are many people who feel they have to change their lives for the better before they give their hearts to Jesus and repent of their sins. But people who feel that way don't understand that Jesus will forgive our sins and give us strength over sin. He knows we have sinned and that we continue to sin. That is why He came to earth. We cannot clean up our own lives. We cannot battle the devil nor can we defeat the power of our own wanton desires. But over time, with our lives surrendered and yielded to Jesus, the power of the sin in our lives begins to diminish. We find that we are no longer slaves to the things we could never control. We actually are able to resist temptation more often than we yield to it. The progress we experience gives us even more faith to resist sin until we are free from it most of the time.

So we should never feel that we are too bad of a person to pray or to ask God to forgive us. The Bible tells us that God demonstrates His own love toward us in that while we were yet sinners, Christ died for us (see Rom. 5:8). It is an amazing love, indeed! While we still struggle with sin, God still loves us, forgives us, and leads on in His plan for us.

God wants us to be confident in our faith. He wants us to know that His love for us is sincere and permanent. His plan for us is solid and tangible. He is tenacious and single-minded toward all of those who surrender to Him.

> *We were God's enemies, but the death of His Son was used to make us God's friends* (Romans 5:10).

It is difficult for many to understand that God desperately wants us to experience all that He has for us. Just think about it. You are reading this because you are hungry for the Lord Jesus in your life. But He is even more hungry for you than you are for Him! He has taken away the only barrier between you and Him—your sin. Now He stands by you waiting for you to respond to His love for you. Jesus said, *"Listen, I stand at the door. I am knocking. If anyone hears My voice and opens the door, I will come inside with him. We will have dinner together. I will give the right to sit with Me at My throne to the person who conquers as I conquered, and as I sat down beside My Father at His throne. The person who has an ear should listen to what the Spirit is saying to the congregations"* (Rev. 3:20-22).

CHANGE OUR ATTITUDE

Our first step is to change the way we think. We realize that we need Him. We admit that we are not doing so well on our own. Therefore, when we change the way we think, we will begin the process of surrendering to our Lord.

NOT TOO HARD

Too many of us believe that God feels we have done too many bad things for Him to want us. Of course religion does not help, as it is the primary purveyor of this thought. In its attempt to keep people in line, religion has chased millions away from the Lord. But the truth is that it is not hard to follow Him. It is not hard to serve the Lord. Jesus said, *"You are tired and have heavy loads. If all of you will come to Me, I will give you rest. Take the job I give you. Learn from Me because I am gentle and humble in heart. You will find rest for your lives. The duty I give you is easy. The load I put upon you is not heavy"* (Matt. 11:28-30).

I don't think He could be clearer than that! We spend too much time looking at our failures and, therefore, condemn ourselves. He looks at our heart's desire to love Him and responds to what we want, not what we do. He will change what we do, but we will never change if we do not allow Him access to our hearts.

Jesus' words are strong enough for us to begin to understand how much He wants to take care of us and make our lives fulfilled and exciting.

So, I tell you, continue asking, and it will be given to you. Keep on searching and you will find. Be knocking, and the door will open for you. You will receive, if you will always ask. You will find, if you continue looking. And the door will open for you, if you continue knocking. Do any of you have a son? What would you do if your son asked you for bread? Would you give him a rock? What if he asked you for a fish? Would you give him a snake? You are evil people, and yet you know how to give good gifts to your children. Surely your heavenly Father knows how to give good things to those people who ask Him (Matthew 7:7-11).

God feels much differently toward you than you have been led to believe. He loves you. He wants you near. Allow your thoughts to be centered on the spiritual reality of His acceptance rather than the earthly things of human struggle and failure. He will change you. You will never succeed if you concentrate on failures. Here is how the apostle Paul says it:

People who follow human nature are thinking about the evil things which human nature wants. People who follow the Spirit are thinking about the things that the Spirit wants. The way human nature thinks is death, but the way the Spirit thinks is life and peace. The way human nature thinks is hatred for God. It doesn't want to put itself under the law of God. It can't! People controlled by human nature cannot please God (Romans 8:5-8).

ADMIT OUR FAILURES

Not centering on our sins does not mean we ignore the places where we know we need to change. For admitting we have struggles is the first step in getting free from the things we hate to do, but find ourselves doing anyway.

In changing our minds, we now understand that He loves us and that He actually wants us. Next, we must confess our sin to the Lord. Of course He already knows our sins and our failures. In fact He knows all our weaknesses. But He also knows our heart and knows our love for Him and our desire to serve Him. So although He knows our sin, we need to admit it to ourselves and to the Lord Jesus. It is a point of true surrender to Him. It gets us on the same page with Him.

If we say, "We have no sin!" then we are only fooling ourselves. The truth is not in us (1 John 1:8).

JESUS WILL CLEANSE OUR HEARTS

How can we be sure that He will forgive us? The answer is quite simple. The Bible tells us that God can be trusted. He never, ever goes against what He has said or what He has promised. When we tell Him our sins, making it clear that we are sorry, His forgiveness is guaranteed.

YOU CAN PRAY IN TONGUES

When I kept things to myself, I felt weakness deep inside me. I moaned all day long. Day and night, You tested me. My strength was gone, as in the summer heat. Then I admitted my sins to You. I did not hide my guilt. I thought: "I will confess my wrongs to the Always-Present One!" And, You did forgive my sins. For this reason, let each one who is godly pray to You while they still can (Psalms 32:3-6).

If we admit our sins, then God will forgive us. We can trust God; He does what is right. He will cleanse us from every evil thing (1 John 1:9).

There is no sin too bad for God to forgive. There is nothing you can do that will cause Him to turn His back on you. His commitment is to work with you, to work in you, and to work for you until you are everything He originally created you to be. His undying commitment is an awesome and solemn promise to everyone who comes to Jesus.

You are my Hiding Place. You protect me from my troubles. You surround me with songs of victory (Psalms 32:7).

ONLY THE BEGINNING

I have helped thousands of people begin or renew their friendship with Jesus. I tell all of them the same thing at this point. This is only the first step. There are steps you need to take every day. There are decisions you need to make. There are issues that need to be addressed. He knows that and He will work with you through each one of them. The Lord will not just make everything disappear, because you hold the keys to your *own* life and the decisions that got you to this point. You also hold the keys to where you will go from here. But He never leaves us alone. His ear is always listening for us to pray. The confession you are about to make releases the power of God to you and everyone around you.

> *The Always-Present One is your Protection. You have made God the Most High your Home. Nothing bad will happen to you. No disaster will come near your home. God will command His angels to take care of you. They will watch over you wherever you go. Their hands will catch you, so that you will not hit your foot against a rock* (Psalms 91:9-12).

All of Heaven is behind you! God has your back, your front, your top…well, He holds you in the palm of His hand.

> *You surround me—in front and in back. You have put Your hand upon me* (Psalms 139:5).

TIME TO PRAY

> Lord Jesus, I know that I am a sinner. I know I do not have the strength to be the person You want me

to be and the person I want to be. Please forgive my sin and cleanse my heart. Come and take control of my life. You are my Savior. You are my Lord. I submit my life to You. Thank You for Your love, for Your forgiveness, and for Your mercy. I look forward to serving you in all I do. Amen.

Wow, congratulations! This is a momentous occasion. You have just begun a journey that will continue for all eternity. You are now exactly where God wants you to be: forgiven, open-hearted, and waiting for the Lord. From this position God will begin the journey with you. He is in you, with you, and holding your hand. As you continue to be open and responsive to the Lord, there is nothing you cannot do.

This, then, is the foundation upon which you will receive the baptism of the Holy Spirit and begin to pray in tongues.

CHAPTER
9

Baptism of the Holy Spirit

On the last and most important day of the festival, Jesus stood and cried out, "If you are thirsty, come to Me and drink! The person who believes in Me will be like the Scripture which says: 'A river of fresh water will flow from his body'" (John 7:37–38).

Now that the Lord has His home inside your heart, there is much He wants to say to you. There is an eternity of dreams He has destined for you. He fully intends to fulfill all His dreams for you. That is what a father does.

As I have said before, when you are baptized with the Holy Spirit, God's Spirit flows to you, through you, and out of you. He will nourish and strengthen you as well as all those around you. Not only does this baptism of the Holy Spirit benefit you and your future, it directly benefits all those you pray for. Your prayer language is about to flow from the very depths of your heart, flowing with life-giving strength and peace.

THE HOLY SPIRIT FOLLOWS FORGIVENESS

It was normal for believers in the early Church to be baptized in the Holy Spirit after they gave their hearts to Jesus. The apostles knew that the Holy Spirit carried the strength and power the believers would need in those difficult days. Paul, especially, worked to be sure believers had the baptism of the Holy Spirit. When the Lord first appeared to him along the road, Paul repented of his sin and became a disciple or follower of Jesus, but he did not get baptized with the Holy Spirit at that time. After he gave his heart to Jesus, the Lord sent a man named Ananias to him in order that he might be baptized with the Holy Spirit.

> *So Ananias left and went to the house of Judas. He put his hands on Saul and said, "Saul, my brother, the Lord Jesus sent me. He is the one you saw on the road when you came here. He sent me, so that you may see again and so*

that you may be filled with the Holy Spirit." Immediately, something which looked like fish scales fell off Saul's eyes. Saul could see again! He got up and was immersed (Acts 9:17-18).

Paul had been blinded that fateful day when Jesus first confronted him, but he regained his sight at the point of surrender when he was filled with the Holy Spirit. It is no wonder then that Paul wanted to be certain that all who had repented of their sins were also filled with the Holy Spirit. He knew the level of power and revelation that would come with this incredible experience.

It is recorded that Paul often confirmed new believers who were, indeed, baptized with the Holy Spirit.

While Apollos was in the city of Corinth, Paul was visiting some places along the northern route to the city of Ephesus. In Ephesus, Paul found some followers of John. Paul asked them, "Did you receive the Holy Spirit when you believed?" These followers answered him, "We have never even heard of a Holy Spirit!" So Paul asked them, "What kind of immersion did you receive?" They said, "It was the immersion which John taught." Paul said, "John immersed people after they changed their hearts. John told people to trust in the One who would come after him. That Person is Jesus." When these followers of John heard this, they were immersed by the authority of the Lord Jesus. Then Paul put his hands on them and the Holy Spirit came upon them. They began speaking different inspired languages and prophesying (Acts 19:1-6).

Turning away from sin is always the first step to a joyful and fulfilling life, but the baptism of the Holy Spirit is a necessary next step to release God's power in every area of life. This should not seem strange. Our soft heart toward the Lord always releases mercy and grace. Humility and dependence on Him will draw God's love and power to you.

Be humble before the Lord and He will lift you up (James 4:10).

Hope never disappoints us, because God's love has been poured into our hearts through the Holy Spirit who was given to us (Romans 5:5).

JESUS—THE BAPTIZER

Whenever you change your hearts, I immerse you in water. But there is One coming later who is more important than I am. I am not worthy to carry His shoes. He will immerse you in the Holy Spirit and in fire! (Matthew 3:11).

Jesus is the one and only Person who can baptize with the Holy Spirit. We can and should lead folks into this experience, helping them to prepare their hearts to respond to the Lord, but Jesus is the one who does the work. When Jesus baptizes with the Holy Spirit, He immerses us with His Spirit. He fills us to overflowing. Just like a cup is filled with water to the point of overflow, Jesus fills us until we overflow with His Presence.

I know that it is hard to imagine, but the Holy Spirit will fill your heart to overflowing! Again, the apostle Paul encourages the church to pray for and expect everything God has for them, even though what God has is far more than any human could imagine:

> *Glory to God! He is able to do so much more than we can even think of or ask for. God uses the power that is working in us. Glory to God among all the people He has called out and in Christ Jesus for all generations forever and ever. Amen* (Ephesians 3:20-21).

FILLED AGAIN AND AGAIN

In fact, there is more good news. After receiving the baptism of the Holy Spirit, the Lord will fill you again and again so you are always equipped with the strength and wisdom you need to do His will every day.

There were many times after their initial experience that the disciples were faced with difficult situations. The Holy Spirit was always faithful to be with them during these times.

The apostle Peter had prayed for a lame man, who was instantly healed. (See Acts 3:1-10.) This caused a great up-roar since the man who was healed was well known to those in Jerusalem, and the religious leaders of the day resisted the disciples and the resurrection of Jesus from the dead. When the leaders of the Synagogue questioned Peter, he was *"…filled with the Holy Spirit. He said to them, 'You elders and leaders of the people: Are you questioning us today about the good thing which was done to this crippled man? Are you asking us who made him well? We want all of you and all the people of Israel to know that this man was made well by the authority of Jesus from Nazareth, the Messiah! Although you nailed Him to the cross, God raised Him from death. This man who was crippled is now well and able to stand here before you because of **Jesus!**'"* (Acts 4:8-10).

A few days later, they were again warned not to teach or preach the Name of Jesus. The disciples gathered together and prayed to the Lord for strength when *"…the place where they were meeting shook. They were all filled with the Holy Spirit and they began to speak God's message without fear"* (Acts 4:31).

The followers of Jesus in Antioch were happy and full of the Holy Spirit (Acts 13:52).

This is why you should not be fools. Instead, try to understand what the Lord wants. Don't get drunk with wine; this leads to wildness. No, be filled with the Spirit (Ephesians 5:17-18).

There are many more Scriptures for you to read in the index of Scriptures on the baptism of the Holy Spirit and praying in tongues. You should read them and meditate on them. I have included the references so you can find the verses in the Bible for yourself. That way you can read all of the verses in context.

JESUS IS READY AND WAITING FOR YOU!

If you are anything like me (and I think you are), your heart is bursting for the Lord and all He has for you. Your time has come. I want to help you to experience the baptism of the Holy Spirit right now. There are a few steps that will prepare your heart and mind to receive as Jesus pours His Spirit into your body, soul, and spirit. He will completely flood every fiber of your being.

First, settle your mind. Focus on the Lord. This is not a time to pray. It is not a time to say anything. Right now, just rest in

Him. Remember that Jesus is the Baptizer. He is the One and only Person who can give you the Holy Spirit and He is with you right now.

I want you to imagine Jesus standing in front of you with one of His hands on your shoulder and the other hand on your head. At this point you need to think about anything that you think will hinder your ability to receive. If there is something that you are doing or have done that you are certain is a sin, it is time to confess that thing to the Lord. It is human nature to try to explain away the things we do that are not pleasing to the Lord. We try to excuse our sin because we are not sure He will forgive us. In some cases, we are positive He cannot forgive us. But the Bible is full of assurances that He *can* and absolutely *will* forgive us.

You Are Safe With Jesus

Here is an amazing statement. It is safe to call a sin a sin. We do not have to ignore what we have done or explain it away as something that is not really a sin. Be honest with the Lord and He will definitely forgive. Isaiah recorded what God said about our sin:

The Always-Present One says, "Come, we will talk these things over. Your sins are red like deep red cloth.

But they can be as white as snow. Your sins are bright red. But you can be white like wool (Isaiah 1:18).

Even King David, who struggled with sin, understood God's love and His absolute forgiveness to a repentant heart. Here is what he says after he confessed to the Lord:

As high as the sky is above the earth, so great is His constant love for those who revere Him. He has taken our sins away from us, as far as the east is from the west. The Always-Present One has mercy upon those who revere Him, as a father has mercy on His children. He knows how we were made. He remembers that we are dust (Psalms 103:11-14).

You are in good hands. You are safe with Jesus. Tell Him you are sorry. Tell Him you don't like the wrong things that you do and that you don't want them in your life. When you confess these things to the Lord, even if they are hard to confess, you will clear your heart and mind to receive the baptism of the Holy Spirit and begin to pray in tongues. The Bible says: *"If we admit our sins, then God will forgive us. We can trust God; He does what is right. He will cleanse us from every evil thing. If we say, 'We have not sinned!' then we are calling God a liar. God's true teaching is not in us"* (1 John 1:9-10).

Confessing your sin allows the Lord to forgive you and clean up your heart so there is nothing that will stand in the way of receiving all God has for you. Now I know we talked about surrendering your life to the Lord earlier. But I want to be sure that there is nothing, to your knowledge, that could stand in the way for receiving.

LET'S PRAY

Have you talked to the Lord? Have you made all the confession you need to make? Does this mean you are ready to move on to receive? Great.

Be sure you are in a quiet place where you will not be interrupted as you pray. This is something you definitely don't want to rush! This is an important and exciting crossroad in your life, so take the time to pray.

You will want to either be alone or have someone with you as you receive. It is up to you, but be certain the person you are with is supportive as well as a seeker. This is not a time to be self-conscious. You need to decide what the best environment is for you: whether to be alone or have someone there who will pray for you. If you want someone with you, it is always best to find someone who has already received the Holy Spirit and already prays in tongues. Just remember, countless millions before you have been in exactly this same place. You may recall how it happened to me. I was alone, so I could speak and sing to my heart's content, no matter how different it sounded to me. I knew it was a miraculous language and you will too.

You may or may not sense the power of the Holy Spirit coming over you. Your feelings have nothing to do with the fact that you asked Jesus to fill you with His Holy Spirit and He answered. That's it. He loves to answer this prayer.

You may want to worship along with a CD or just sing to the Lord with a favorite song of worship. Keep your spirit open and allow yourself to be abandoned to Him and His Presence. As you worship, you will begin to sense a welling up of His Spirit from deep within your spirit. Allow this to happen to you; it is a good thing. It is the filling of the Holy Spirit. As you sense strange sounds, go ahead and utter them out loud. You are either alone or with someone who is supportive, so it doesn't matter what it sounds like.

So let's pray: "Lord Jesus, You know my heart. You know all about me. You know that I love you, need you, and want all You have for me. Lord Jesus, please baptize me with Your Holy Spirit. Fill me completely from the top of my head down to my feet. Fill my body, my soul, and my spirit with Your Holy Spirit. Thank You, Lord Jesus. I receive Your Spirit into my heart, into my life. So be it, Lord."

It is time to stop reading and start worshiping. These verses from the Bible will help you get started:

O God, You are my God I want to follow You. My soul thirsts for You. My body yearns for You, in a dry, empty land where there is no water. So I have beheld You in the sanctuary. I have seen Your strength and Your glory. Your constant love is better than life. I will praise You loudly. So I will praise You as long as I live (Psalms 63:1-3).

Sing a new song to the Always-Present One. Sing to the Always-Present One, all the earth. Sing to the Always-Present One. Praise His Name. Every day, tell the good news that He saves us. Tell the nations about His glory. Proclaim His miracles among all peoples. Why? Because the Always-Present One is great; He should be highly praised. He should be revered more than all the so-called gods. All the gods of the ethnic groups are only idols. But the Always-Present One created the skies. Glory and majesty are in His presence. Power and beauty are in His sanctuary. Assign to the Always-Present One, all you clans of various ethnic groups. Assign glory and power to the One Who Is Always Present. Assign the glory owed to His Name. Bring an offering and come into His courtyards. Worship the Always-Present One with the beauty of holiness (Psalms 96:1-9).

See you in the next chapter.

CHAPTER
10

New Beginnings

I ndeed, this is a new beginning for you. Now the Holy Spirit is free within you to work like He has never been able to work before. It is not a matter of feelings. It is not a matter of emotion. It is a matter of fact. For now, *"…God is the One who is working in you. How? He causes you to want to do what pleases Him"* (Phil. 2:13).

Remember that God gave you free will. Because of that, He will not invade your *space*. He will not force Himself on you, as your free will is what makes you different from all other living creatures. He wants your love and devotion to be natural, born out of your personal desire to want to be with Him. So He will not work where He has not been given the express permission to work. That is why this is such an important step for you. When you asked the Lord to fill you with His Spirit, you asked Him to possess you—body, soul, and spirit. You yielded yourself to Him, and He responded to the sincerity of your heart, as He will always do. Every time you pray in tongues, you are reminding yourself that your life is not your own, that you have submitted it to the Holy Spirit. Your prayer tongue bypasses your brain and the resistance of your will because you do not want your doubt or fear to interfere with God's work within your life. Every time you pray in tongues, you are renewing your commitment to allow God's will to overrule your will.

New Beginning

There will be times of doubt and uncertainty. There will be plenty of times when you will not feel His Presence. These are all natural in the growth and personal maturing process. Yielding to the Holy Spirit is a new beginning in many ways. It is as though you are a child all over again. This is such a good example because you are now discovering a new dimension. You are discovering a whole new reality, the reality of Spirit and all-God. Jesus described it this way: *"I am telling you the truth: If you don't change and become like little children, you will never enter the kingdom of heaven. The person* who humbles himself like this little child is the most important one in the kingdom of heaven" (Matt. 18:3-4). *"Let the children come to Me. Don't stop them, because the kingdom of heaven belongs to people who are like these children"* (Matt. 19:14).

NEW DISCOVERIES

Little children are full of wonder and awe about everything. Their enthusiasm about life is invigorating. My parents loved for our five sons to visit them. They said that the boys reminded them how wonderful life is. Cathy's mom loved the hustle, bustle, and noise of grandkids whirling through the house like hurricanes. I have to admit as well, *our* grandkids are an absolute delight. They are so enthralled with life-changing discoveries! They love everything about life and get up too early in the morning in the anticipation of what the day will show them.

Our son Joel was by far the most curious and inquisitive of all our sons. When he was born, instead of crying the moment he was born, Joel said, "I'm bored. What can we do?" It is natural and essential that the mind of a child should have an insatiable hunger to learn. A child is so open, so innocent, so vulnerable. He is like a chick just hatched from an egg. He is in the nest with his eyes closed and his mouth open! Such is the trusting nature of a child. He will rely implicitly on his parents and trust them to a fault to take perfect care of him.

Your new life in the realm of all-God is the same thing. God made us to be trusting children. He wants us to approach this newfound realm with curiosity and anticipation. He wants to teach us all about the new things of the Holy Spirit and to trust in Jesus. We *can* trust the Lord. We can trust the Name of Jesus and the things we see and hear in His Name. Check out these words of Jesus:

> *Do any of you have a son? What would you do if your son asked you for bread? Would you give him a rock? What if he asked you for a fish? Would you give him a snake? You are evil people, and yet you know how to give good gifts to your children. Surely your heavenly Father knows how to give good things to those people who ask Him* (Matthew 7:9-11).

> *The Always-Present One's constant love never ends. His mercies never stop. They are fresh every morning. O God, Your faithfulness is great* (Lamentations 3:22-23).

GOD IS EVERYWHERE, GOD IS HERE

You will soon sense the Presence of the Lord in a new way. The very possibility of being filled with His Spirit is already happening to you. The nearness of the Lord is an experience like no other on the earth. You already know in theory that God is everywhere. From a small child, most of us have understood that no matter where we go, how we feel, or what trouble we are in, God is already there. This so important because it is basic to all we believe. We know God is everywhere because He told us He is everywhere.

Most people never think twice about praying, no matter where they are or what circumstances they are in. You could be flying over the ocean at 600 mph in a Boeing 777 jet that is seven miles above the earth and God still hears you. You can be in a wilderness camping and He is there with you. You can be in a war zone, alone in your home, or working as an astronaut on the moon, and He is still there with you.

We know He is with us. King David often found himself in places that were far from the posh comforts of the palace; yet he found the reality of God no matter where he was. David knew God was with him as he was keeping the sheep on a desolate hill. He knew God was with him as he was betrayed by his brother. Whether he was in his palace or running for his life and hiding in a cave, he knew God was there. David described his experiences this way:

O One Who Is Always Present, You have examined me. You know everything there is about me. You know when I sit down and when I get up. From a distance, You understand my thoughts. You know where I go and where I lie down. You are familiar with all of my ways. O One Who Is Always Present, even before I say a word, behold, You already know what I am going to say. You surround me—in front and in back. You have put Your hand upon me. Such knowledge is too wonderful for me. It is more than I can understand. Where could I go to get away from Your Spirit? Nowhere. Where could I run from Your presence? Nowhere. If I were to go up to the skies, You are there. If I were to lie down where the dead are, behold You are there. If I were to get up at dawn, or settle in beyond the sea, even there Your hand would guide me. You would hold me tight with Your right hand. If I were to think, "The darkness will surely hide me. The light around me will turn into night," even the darkness would not be dark to You. The night would be as light as the day. To You, darkness and light are the same (Psalms 139:1-12).

But there is another level of experience with the Presence of the Lord that King David enjoyed. This is the manifest Presence of the Lord. This experience is when the Presence is so strong that you can feel it in one or more of the five senses. This is not the intellectual knowledge of His Presence; it is the experiential knowledge of His Presence. You know He is near because you feel Him. You know that you know He is with you. Again, King David describes it this way:

You surround me—in front and in back. You have put Your hand upon me. Such knowledge is too wonderful for me. It is more than I can understand (Psalms 139:5-6).

This inner knowledge of His Presence is truly our comfort, our peace, and our hiding place from the storms of life. It is by far the greatest advantage we have as believers in Jesus. God is not just with us. He is in us.

You yourselves know that you are God's temple sanctuary. Don't you know that the Spirit of God lives in you? (1 Corinthians 3:16).

But if the Spirit of Him who raised Jesus from the dead dwells in you, He who raised Christ Jesus from the dead will also give life to your mortal body through His Spirit who indwells you (see Rom. 8:11).

WE GROW DAY BY DAY

This new and interactive relationship with the Lord is the beginning of a fresh time of growth in knowledge, strength, and understanding in the ways of God. He will work within our hearts 24/7 to make us everything He wants us to be. Of course He has always worked in us, but now that we have yielded to Him in a deeper way, we can expect to notice an accelerated activity of God in our lives.

Again, your new sensitivity and your deeper yielding to Him will help you actually know what He is doing. You will also be more inclined to work with Him as you understand and sense His work within you.

> *I feel sure of this one thing: The One who began a good work among you will continue it until it is finished, when Christ Jesus comes* (Philippians 1:6).

> *...because God is the One who is working in you. How? He causes you to want to do what pleases Him* (Philippians 2:13).

> *This is why we continually thank God: When you received God's message that you heard from us, you accepted it as the true message of God, not a human message. It is working in you believers* (1 Thessalonians 2:13).

> *We are what God made. In Christ Jesus we have been created for doing good deeds. God prepared these good deeds long ago, so that we could live by them* (Ephesians 2:10).

UNION WITH GOD

This kind of cooperation with the Lord is the essence of our union with Him. It is the substance of fellowship and intimacy. The Lord sees the very deepest issues of the heart and works to bring wholeness and freedom. We begin to see and understand the desires of His heart, so we yield ourselves to Him for the purpose of His desire. Maybe for the first time in your life, you will feel as though you are truly walking with God.

Our union with Him will change everything we have ever thought and challenge everything we have learned. Union with Him is why I call our newfound relationship with Him "interactive." We are no longer praying into the air to someone we know is there but are not at all sure will hear or care about what we pray for.

In the same way, He is no longer striving with us as we naturally resist Him. We resisted because we did not understand that He was working on our behalf. Instead, the relationship is now interactive. We see Him in our lives and so we yield. When we yield, the work of the Holy Spirit is easier, since we are cooperating. Progress can be seen and God's activity in our lives becomes more obvious. That is as it should be; for He is the One who reveals Jesus to us and is the Teacher to whom we all turn and yield.

God gave you a gift. You still have this gift inside you. You don't need anyone to teach you. The gift that He gave you teaches you about everything. This gift is true;

it is not false. Because of this, continue to live in God, just as His gift taught you (1 John 2:27).

THE JOURNEY

The bottom line here is simple. We are on a journey. We are changing from earthly people to spiritual people. We are becoming *God-conscious*. We are becoming newly aware of a realm we did not know had such power. We are learning that things are not always as they appear; that the five senses cannot interpret the things of the spirit realm, since they cannot even sense them. We are discovering new levels of reality, trust, joy, fulfillment, and love. The best thing of all is that this is only the beginning. It will take a lifetime to explore the wonders and glory of the Lord Jesus. But this is a compelling motivation for you. I see your heart, and I know you are just like me.

INDEX OF SCRIPTURES ON THE HOLY SPIRIT AND PRAYING IN TONGUES

*T*hen Peter answered, "Change your hearts and each one of you must be immersed by the authority of Jesus the Messiah, so that your sins may be forgiven. Then you will receive the gift of the Holy Spirit. This promise is for **you** and for your children. It is also for people who are far away, for everyone whom the Lord our God may call." Peter was warning them with many other words; he was encouraging them, saying, "Be saved from this twisted generation of people!" Then those people who accepted what Peter said were immersed. On that day, about 3,000 people were added to the group of believers (Acts 2:38-41).

The apostles were still in Jerusalem. They heard that the people of Samaria had accepted God's message. So, the apostles sent Peter and John to the people in Samaria. When Peter and John arrived, they prayed for the Samaritan believers to receive the Holy Spirit. (These people had been immersed by the authority of the Lord Jesus, but the Holy Spirit had not yet come down on any of them.) The two apostles put their hands on the people. Then the people received the Holy Spirit (Acts 8:14-17).

*While Peter was still speaking these words, the Holy Spirit came upon all those people who were listening to his speech. The Jewish believers who came with Peter were amazed. They were shocked because the gift of the Holy Spirit was poured out on people who were **not** Jewish. These Jewish believers heard them speaking different inspired languages and praising God. Then Peter said, "Can we refuse to allow these people to be immersed in water? They have received the Holy Spirit the same as we did!"* (Acts 10:44-47)

After I began my speech, the Holy Spirit came upon them, the same as He did upon us in the beginning. Then I remembered the words of the Lord Jesus when He used to say: "John immersed people in water, but you will be immersed in the Holy Spirit!" God gave the same gift to these people that He gave to us who believed in the Lord Jesus, the Messiah. So, could I stop God? (Acts 11:15-17)

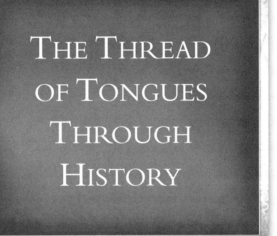

THE THREAD OF TONGUES THROUGH HISTORY

*This promise is for **you** and for your children. It is also for people who are far away, for everyone whom the Lord our God may call* (Acts 2:39).

THE TORCH OF THE HOLY SPIRIT

There is a saying we often hear when a situation looks bleak: Things are "hanging by a thread." Throughout history things did become very bleak, indeed. It seemed as though everything concerning the fire of the Holy Spirit in the Church and the people of God in general, hung by a thread. Of course, that is because we seem to judge everything according to what we see, not by what the Lord is hiding in the hearts of those who had yielded to Him. For when we explore what was happening among the early believers, we find that the fire of the Holy Spirit burned brightly. These believers carried the torch of His Presence from one generation to another.

THE TIME OF JESUS

The Jewish nation was under the thumb of the Roman Empire. But it was religious leaders that gave our Lord His biggest problems. These men were as Jesus described them to be: *"a brood of vipers,"* (see Matt. 12:34; 23:33 NKJV) and *"whited sepulchers…full of dead men's bones"* (see Matt. 23:27 KJV). Because they feared for their own positions and their own authority, they resisted the work of the Holy Spirit and thus did their best to stop the will of God of the Ages.

But in the midst of this seemingly hopeless time, there remained a thread of faithful believers who sought their God and wanted fellowship with Him more than they loved life itself. They carried the torch of the Holy Spirit and the testimony of Jesus through the most difficult circumstances. These included Mary, the Mother of Christ; her cousin Elizabeth, along with Zachariah, who served faithfully in the

Temple as a priest; the saints who were continually praying, such as Anna, a prophetess in her old age; and Simeon who, by the Holy Spirit, prophesied when his eyes saw God's salvation in the Christ Child. These were saints of old who, despite the darkness of the times, bore a faithful witness to God according to the Scriptures.

Yes, the Church Jesus was building continued from the time of Christ and through succeeding generations. Though at times seeming to be "hanging by a thread" from persecutions, apostasy, heresies, and ecclesiastical corruption, they found a way to keep the fire of the Spirit alive even to our present day.

TRACING THE THREAD

We can trace this "thread" of the life in the Spirit throughout history. Their legacy and courage are indisputably clear. The Book of Acts records the events of the Day of Pentecost. It records the first great outpouring of the Holy Spirit with the accompanying effects of speaking in tongues and prophecy. During that first-century Church era, it was the apostle John who taught one of the Church fathers, Polycarp (A.D. 69-156), to be a faithful witness and testimony to the Living Christ. In turn, Polycarp taught his pupil, Iranaeus (A.D. 130-200), who became Bishop of Lyons in Gaul

(France). This Iranaeus, of the third generation from John, made specific references in his writings of "many brethren in the Church, who possess prophetic gifts, and who through the Spirit speak all kinds of languages, and bring to light for the general benefit the hidden things of men, and declare the mysteries of God."[1]

It is interesting that down through the years in Lyons, France, the faithful disciples of Christ and followers of the teachings of the apostles, including the saints, both the known and unknown kept the thread of the Spirit alive. Then in A.D. 1174, God called a man named Peter Waldo. Through a powerful conversion to the faith, Waldo proclaimed by the power of the Spirit the authority of Scripture, and lay preaching was revived in the midst of ecclesiastical corruption. The Waldenses movement was born and became a forerunner to the Reformers who were to come.

It was another Church Father, Tertullian (A.D. 160-220), who kept a record of the activity of the Holy Spirit in the second and into the third century. In A.D. 207, he wrote specifically of the spiritual gift of interpretation of tongues being practiced in his day among the people. Also, during the third century, Novatian (A.D. 200-258), the Second Antipope, quoted from the Scriptures and spoke consistently regarding the power gifts. He described "tongues, powers of healing, and discerning of spirits and other gifts of the charismata."[2]

During the fourth century, Hilary of Poitiers (A.D. 300-368) wrote of the "gifts of speaking or interpreting divers kinds of tongues." This early torchbearer stated emphatically concerning the gifts of the Holy Spirit that, "Clearly these are the Church's agents of ministry and work of whom the Body of Christ consists; and God has ordained them."[3]

Beginning in the fourth century, however, the record of the flame of tongues grows very faint. But God was faithful, who by the Holy Spirit continued the thread by causing to rise up at that time Augustine of Hippo (A.D. 354-430). He wrote concerning the believers of his day that they "exult and rejoice, being as it were filled with so great joy, that they cannot express it in words, then turn from actual words, and proceed to sounds of jubilation. The jubilee is a sound signifying that the heart labors with which it cannot utter…that the heart may rejoice without words, and the boundless extent of joy may have no limits of syllables."[4]

From the fifth century to the first millennium, the record of speaking in tongues and other gifts is particularly silent. With the Fall of Rome in A.D. 476, the Roman Empire collapsed which led to political anarchy and great distress among the people. Known only to God are the faithful unknown ones who were true to God in the midst of darkness and apostasy. We do know from history that there were many groups who ascribed to the doctrines of the apostles and preached the Gospel in truth. Out of them came, in later years, the fruit of their faithfulness.

The flame of the Spirit appeared again in Germany at the turn of the millennium when Hildgard of Bingen (A.D. 1098-1179) both spoke and sang in tongues.[5] The spiritual songs that were wondrously given by the grace working within her were regarded by contemporaries as "concerts in the Spirit." From this sickly child, given to the Church by her parents as a tithe to God, came forth by God's grace one who was blessed and used by her heavenly Father for His Kingdom.

In the 14th century in Bohemia, the Moravians kept the flame alive by commonly breaking into what a contemporary described as "exuberant evacuations of the Spirit."[6] Known for their unbroken continuance in prayer for 100 years, as well as their missionary activity, the Moravians went forth in the power of the Spirit with the gifts of the Spirit being evident in their witness. Being led by the Spirit and filled with His power and the gifts of the Spirit, these torch carriers lit fires in many parts of the world and still shine brightly, even to this day.

During the 1600s the Camisards, (the Huguenots) were known to speak in tongues. These peasants of Cevennes, a region in south central France, were of tremendous influence among the people, extending into England and Spain. Their writings were influential with later Protestant sects, such as the Shakers and Quakers.

The Quakers were founded by George Fox (1624-1691) and were known as the Society of Friends. The early Quakers make mention of speaking in tongues in their meetings. Edward Burrough wrote: "We spoke with new tongues, as the Lord gave us utterance, and His Spirit led us."[7]

In the 1800s in the Church of Scotland, Edward Irving wrote of the gift of tongues being powerfully evident and "a great instrument for personal edification, however mysterious it may seem to us."[8]

Indeed, as the apostle Paul states in First Corinthians 14:2, *"Anyone who is speaking in an inspired language is not communicating to men, but to God. No one understands him. He is speaking the secrets of God by inspiration."*

The 19th and 20th centuries witnessed a new and fresh outpouring of the Spirit in the Church. The Pentecostal and Charismatic Renewals are a testimony that the thread, although slim for a time, became not just a thread, but a chord of great power and a fiery testimony to the living Christ. This flaming torch of His Presence burns brightly today and is recorded for the ages to come. This, by the way, is part of the mission of Destiny Image Publishers. We have published over 1,000 titles and printed millions of books that will, for the centuries to come, tell of all that God has done during this time of history.

BE PART OF THIS MIRACULOUS THREAD

The historical record of speaking and praying in tongues is clear evidence of the unceasing Presence of the grace *(charis)* of God in the Church. God's faithfulness to call, anoint with the Holy Spirit, and send forth those chosen by Him to keep the flame of the Holy Spirit alive in the Church has been proven again and again. The wonderfully good news is that now in this present time you can be part of the faith of the apostles and saints who have gone before. You, too, can speak and pray in tongues as the Spirit fills you and moves you in the years to come. The ability to speak mysteries to your heavenly Father in your own new prayer language of the Spirit has a long heritage of power and fruitfulness. May the thread be continued in you.

ENDNOTES

1. Irenaeus, *Against Heresies,* Book V, Chapter VI. Quoted in "Glossolalia," *Wikipedia,* http://en.wikipedia.org/wiki/Glossolalia#Church. History (accessed June 3, 2009).

2. http://en.wikipedia.org/wiki/Glossolalia# Church.History_.28A.D_100_to_500.29 Note 41 (accessed June 3, 2009).

3. Hilary of Poitiers, *On the Trinity*, Vol 8 Chap 33.

4. http://en.wikipedia.org/wiki/Glossolalia# Church.History_.28A.D_100_to_500.29 Note 48.

5. "Glossolalia," *Wikipedia*, http://en.wikipedia.org/ wiki/Glossolalia#Church.History (accessed June 3, 2009).

6. Stanley M. Burgess, "Medieval and Modern Western Churches," *Initial Evidence,* ed. Gary B. McGee (Peabody, MA: Hendrickson, 1991), 32.

7. Epistle to the Reader by Edward Burrough, prefixed to George Fox, *The Great Mystery of the Great Whore Unfolded* and *Antichrist's Kingdom Revealed Unto Destruction* (London: Thomas Simmons, 1659).

8. Edward Irving and Gavin Carlyle, *The Collected Writings of Edward Irving* (London: Alexander Strahan, 1865), 548.

About the Author

Don Nori Sr. is the founder of Destiny Image Publishers and MercyPlace Ministries. MercyPlace Ministries is a non-profit renewal and revival ministry whose focus is to bring Jesus to a world that desperately needs Him.

www.mercyplace.com

If you would like to order copies of this book or messages
preached by Don Nori Sr. visit

www.destinyimage.com

If you would like to contact Don Nori Sr.
regarding a speaking engagement,
please e-mail him at
publisher@destinyimage.com
or contact his assistant,
Alex Sadowski at **717-532-3040 ext. 124**

Additional copies of this book and other
book titles from DESTINY IMAGE are
available at your local bookstore.

Call toll-free: 1-800-722-6774.

Send a request for a catalog to:

Destiny Image® Publishers, Inc.

P.O. Box 310
Shippensburg, PA 17257-0310

*"Speaking to the Purposes of God for This
Generation and for the Generations to Come."*

**For a complete list of our titles,
visit us at www.destinyimage.com.**